# Linguistics

Polity's *Why It Matters* series

In these short and lively books, world-leading thinkers make the case for the importance of their subjects and aim to inspire a new generation of students.

Lynn Hunt, *History*
Tim Ingold, *Anthropology*
Neville Morley, *Classics*
Alexander B. Murphy, *Geography*
Geoffrey K. Pullum, *Linguistics*

Geoffrey K. Pullum

———

# Linguistics

## Why It Matters

polity

First published in 2018 by Polity Press

Polity Press
65 Bridge Street
Cambridge CB2 1UR, UK

Polity Press
101 Station Landing
Suite 300
Medford, MA 02155, USA

ISBN-13: 978-1-5095-3075-5
ISBN-13: 978-1-5095-3076-2 (pb)

A catalogue record for this book is available from the British Library.

Typeset in 11 on 15 Sabon by Servis Filmsetting Ltd, Stockport, Cheshire
Printed and bound in the UK by CPI Group (UK) Ltd, Croydon

The publisher has used its best endeavours to ensure that the URLs for external websites referred to in this book are correct and active at the time of going to press. However, the publisher has no responsibility for the websites and can make no guarantee that a site will remain live or that the content is or will remain appropriate.

Every effort has been made to trace all copyright holders, but if any have been inadvertently overlooked the publisher will be pleased to include any necessary credits in any subsequent reprint or edition.

For further information on Polity, visit our website: politybooks.com

# Contents

*Preface*                                          vi

1  What Makes Us Human                       1
2  How Sentences Work                        19
3  Words, Meaning, and Thought               39
4  Language and Social Life                  66
5  Machines That Understand Us               83
Conclusion                                   121

*Notes on Further Reading*                   124
*Index*                                      130

# Preface

This book is about the point of studying human language scientifically, and what importance that study has for broader concerns. The relevant scientific study is known as linguistics, but I construe the term very broadly, to include everything from practical applied concerns to abstract mathematical work on language structure, plus research specialities like phonetics and pragmatics, and hybrid disciplines like psycholinguistics and sociolinguistics. Sometimes I speak in the plural, and refer to the linguistic sciences.

Linguistics is not at all the same as the study of particular languages or their literatures. Some linguists are extraordinarily talented at learning and speaking foreign languages (knowing linguistics actually helps with that), but linguistics is not about learning or using or translating languages.

# Preface

It's about getting a general theoretical understanding of their nature, and developing techniques for analysing and describing them.

I'm not trying to give any sort of introduction to linguistics in this relatively short book; plenty of other books do that. What I'm trying to do is to survey just a few topics that I feel make a clear case for saying that linguistics is not just an intellectually intriguing academic subject but a practically important one. I have done what I could, but I'm sure the number of linguists who feel I have picked exactly the right topics will be approximately zero. You will be able to confirm by chatting to any linguists you might meet; I encourage you to do so – and ask them which topics they would have chosen.

Linguistics is a young subject. Its history as an established academic subject taught in universities doesn't really go back much before World War II. The Linguistics Association of Great Britain was not founded until 1959, and the Linguistic Society of America is only thirty-five years older. The subject never figured in secondary schools until quite recent reforms in Britain, and before 1965 it wasn't even available at undergraduate level in British universities. Lots of well-educated people know virtually nothing about the subject. If this book does a little bit to encourage someone to consider taking up the study of linguistics at university, or even just taking one class in it, I shall be well satisfied.

It was my good luck to discover in the late 1960s what linguistics was, and that it had become available as an undergraduate subject at the University of York. The BA course I did there was the start of a lifetime of academic enjoyment and satisfaction. I have never for a second regretted switching into linguistics after five years in my first career (for those years I worked as a professional rock musician). I still think the linguistic sciences have great and largely underappreciated significance for society.

My continuing study of linguistics has been much aided by the colleagues I am fortunate enough to have at the University of Edinburgh. Many have helped, but I should specifically thank Melinda Wood for information about Hawaiian, Jerry Sadock for Greenlandic Inuit material in Chapter 3, Rebecca Wheeler for insights and references regarding Chapter 4, and Mark Steedman for fruitful discussions and some nice examples in Chapter 5. In addition, I owe a debt to Justin Dyer for expert and enormously helpful editing work on the manuscript and to Jim Donaldson for help with the proofs.

In a book as short as this I cannot possibly give full background information and bibliographical references. I have noted sources for a few key points in the notes at the end, and details about other topics will often be easily found through a web search, but anyone who is unable to locate a primary source that they need should email me: **linguistics@politybooks.com** is the address to use.

# 1

# What Makes Us Human

An extraterrestrial zoologist observing our planet's wildlife a few hundred thousand years ago might well have been puzzled. The strange, soft-skinned, almost hairless primates that had emerged over the previous million years did not initially look like a good evolutionary bet, but they were doing incredibly well. Despite lacking the fangs, claws, or protective carapaces that other animals needed for safety, they were thriving. And they were developing skills and practices that the planet had never seen in any animal before. They lived in socially organized bands; nurtured and controlled fire to keep warm at night, deter predators, and cook food; planned and organized collaborative hunting; manufactured tools and weapons, sometimes with the aid of other tools; and developed practices like caring for the sick and burying the dead.

Their exploration of the planet grew steadily more ambitious. They populated not only the entire African continent but also the gigantic Eurasian land mass to the north and east. Ambrose Bierce quipped (before either of the twentieth century's great world wars) that although humans seem addicted to extermination of their own species as well as others, nonetheless humankind 'multiplies with such insistent rapidity as to infest the whole habitable earth and Canada.' As generations passed, they steadily became more and more expert at making complex tools, weapons, ornaments, pictures, sculptures, clothes, and boats. They had found a new way to pass knowledge and skills down the generations, completely transcending biological transmission of physical traits through genetic inheritance. We don't know when it happened: maybe 100,000 or 200,000 years ago, and possibly hundreds of thousands of years earlier; but at some time in the prehistoric past *Homo sapiens* (or quite possibly their immediate ancestors, *Homo erectus*) had developed language.

Today there are roughly 7 billion of us humans. We are the most important animals on earth, if only because of our unparalleled power to modify and perhaps destroy the planet's very capacity to support life. Animals of other species do all sorts of clever things, and alter their environments in many ways, but it's nothing comparable to what humans do. The complexity of human thought, behaviour, technology, and environmental modification is of an entirely different kind.

The aspects of human life that make our species unique depend in numerous ways on the special human ability to use language. For anyone who thinks it is important to understand what humans are like and why, a scientific comprehension of the capacity for language is essential. Linguistics is the scientific field devoted to achieving that understanding.

## *What Languages Are*

What exactly do I mean by a 'language'? In a sense the whole discipline of linguistics is devoted to a long-term project of properly answering that question by giving a full theory of the nature of human languages, the things they share, and the ways in which they differ. But as a rough starting point, human languages are structured systems for making articulated thoughts fully explicit both internally (mentally) and externally (in a form perceptible to other humans), and linguistics studies all components of such systems, together with the ways in which they are used.

It is extremely common for people to take 'language' and 'communication' to be the same thing. In this book, however, they are never equated. They are clearly distinct in that each is found in the absence of the other. Most communication, even between humans, has nothing to do with language (think of frowning, winking, shrugging, grinning, eyebrow-raising, caressing, or glaring). Some of it isn't even voluntary (blushing, limping, trembling). And conversely, lots of the use we make of language involves no communication in any reasonable sense. Think of someone silently planning a speech that they will never give, or checking a document for wording errors, or silently reflecting on whether *likely* has exactly the same meaning as *probable*.

All animals communicate, but only humans have languages in the sense that is relevant for this book. That doesn't mean I disapprove of talk about the language of music, flowers, art, or architecture. It's just that when we get down to brass tacks, these metaphorical extensions of the term 'language' should be ignored, because they will only encourage confusion. When I talk about language I will never be referring to concertos, carnations, collages, or cupolas.

Let me get just a little more specific about languages. The systems that linguists study connect virtually unbounded numbers of sentence meanings (arbitrarily complex thoughts) to external realizations, in a medium-independent way (a given sentence can be presented in either written or spoken form). Thus the subject matter for linguists extends from the study of the ways in which speech sounds are made (phonetics) to the study of how meaningful sentences are used in context to convey implicit meanings (pragmatics). Sentences can instruct or query or exhort or signal emotion, and crucially they can express claims, either true and false, and can be used not only externally, for communication or easing of social interaction, but also internally, for reasoning.

Consider a specific sentence like *Everybody seems to be leaving*. You don't need to utter it aloud; you can just think it. You can also privately and internally figure out its logical consequences; for example, it implies that apparently nobody is planning to stay. It could provide grounds for thinking that pretty soon the place will be empty. You could make it audible by saying it out loud, or make it visible by writing it down (in lower-case letters, or capital letters, or for that matter in Morse code), but you don't have to. It's still a sentence. And crucially, **you can do any or all of these things without being in a situation where the statement could conceivably be true.** The sentence doesn't just pop up involuntarily in your mouth when everyone does actually seem to be leaving. You can consider the sentence and grasp its meaning whether it's true right now or not.

Other animals show no signs of being able to do anything of this sort. Various cases have been reported of animals (from monkeys to prairie dogs) that produce warning cries when predators are spotted, and make different sounds for different types of predators – one call for a snake on the ground, another for an eagle in the air, and so on. But they produce these calls involuntarily when a predator is noticed, and they never use the calls for anything else. It's nothing like what you, as a speaker of a human language, can do. You can wonder aloud about who would win in a fight between an eagle and a snake, without there being any eagles or snakes in the vicinity. No monkey can do that.

That's not to say animals are unintelligent. Dogs, in particular, have a wonderful social ability: more than any other animal, they use their intelligence to attempt to figure out what we're paying attention to and what we might be planning. They have admirable memory powers, too. A border collie named

Rico (1994–2004) was trained to fetch any of about 200 specific named toys on command. In fact, if given an unfamiliar name ('Fetch the glimp!') Rico would run and fetch a previously unnamed toy, if there was one, assuming the new word was its name (an apparent word-learning behaviour known as 'fast mapping').

However, this was entirely the result of intensive training and supplying of rewards. Rico only responded to the owner's fetch commands, and responded solely by running to fetch the named toy. Everything was task-based and in the moment. As the psycholinguist Paul Bloom noted, humans can use a noun like *sock* in other ways than by running to the bedroom to fetch one in order to get a snack as a reward. Complaining about having lost one, for example, or asking whether it's time to go out and buy some. That kind of word use is the province of humans alone. And it forms just one small part of the array of human abilities that linguistics seeks to understand.

### *Languages of the World*

About 7,000 distinct languages are in use among human communities today. I say 'about', because making the number precise is not really possible. No sharp scientific distinction can be drawn between two slightly different forms of one language and two distinct but very closely related languages. The distinctions are only assumed to be really clear where social and political facts draw suitable lines.

We take Flemish and Dutch to be different languages, because of the Belgium–Netherlands border, though they're extremely similar. We imagine that people on either side of the Netherlands–Germany border speak different languages, when in fact the local rural dialects on either side hardly differ at all. Everyday Urdu and Hindi are almost identical except for minor pronunciation differences (though they diverge in learned and culture-specific vocabulary), but their Pakistani and Indian speakers very firmly insist that they are different languages. This suggests we may be overcounting languages.

But in other ways we may be undercounting. We take lowland Scots to be just English with a Scottish accent, but linguists generally regard Scots and English to be separate languages. From a distance, it might look as if the language of Italy is Italian, but closer examination reveals that it has eight or nine different closely related Romance languages. Even in Milan and Genoa the form of utterances is not quite the same, never mind in Venice and Palermo.

So saying that someone is using a human language is clear enough, but saying that one person is using the same language as another is not; it is inherently vague. However, if we assume that the undercounting and overcounting roughly cancel each other out, 7,000 languages is probably the right sort of number to assume.

But if that many languages were shared out equally between 7 billion people, we would expect each language to have about a million speakers. Instead we find an extraordinary imbalance.

English is used by one to two billion people: 400 million native speakers and way over a billion others who either have it as a second language or use it regularly as a foreign language. But thousands of the world's languages – especially in Australia, the Americas, and the Pacific – are on the edge of extinction, spoken only by tiny numbers of old people.

Language extinction is of concern because neither languages nor species tend to come back once they've died off. If you ever wanted to see a dodo or a thylacine, it's too late. It's the same with your chances of hearing Galilean Aramaic (Jesus' language) or the language of the Plains Apache Indians: those languages have no native speakers left. And the pace of language extinction is swift and increasing. The time from one language extinction to the next is now about two weeks on average.

One of the ways in which work in linguistics has served traditional societies is through promoting and assisting language revival efforts. Hawaiian, for example, was for a time almost extinct. Only on the small 'forbidden island' of Ni'ihau is Hawaiian the language of daily life for everyone. Ni'ihau is owned by a single family, the Robinsons, who have always encouraged the preservation of the Hawaiian language and culture. The island's population fluctuates, but is never more than a few dozen people, nearly all of whom regularly travel to Kaua'i, where there is radio and TV and everyone speaks English. Around the year 2000, only 0.1% of the population of the state of Hawaii spoke Hawaiian.

But there has been a remarkable change over the past two or three decades in the other islands. An excellent grammar and dictionary of Hawaiian were produced by the linguists Samuel Elbert and Margaret Kawena Pukui in the 1970s and 1980s. Public interest grew in educating children through the medium of the Hawaiian language. Daily radio broadcasts of the news in Hawaiian were introduced. Today thousands of people in the state of Hawaii are learning and regularly using Hawaiian; thousands of children have completed all twelve grades of primary and secondary schooling in full-immersion Hawaiian-language schools; and the University of Hawaii has changed its regulations to permit even PhD dissertations to be submitted in Hawaiian.

The story of Hawaiian might have been very different, for success in revivals of moribund languages is highly unusual. The revival of the virtually extinct Medieval Hebrew to form Modern Hebrew is sometimes described as the only truly successful case. The modest movements to revive Cornish (extinct since the eighteenth century) and Manx (extinct since the death of Ned Maddrell in 1974) involve very few people, and it is not at all clear that government support of other Celtic languages like Irish and Welsh is boosting the number of speakers. Many linguists, however, are interested in assisting efforts to accomplish such revivals, and provide valuable expertise.

Linguistics is tied to the issue of language extinction in two directions. First, the only way for linguistic scientists to study the full range of possibilities for human linguistic ability is to develop a thorough understanding of all the examples of languages available. With each one lost, some information becomes forever unknowable. Thus saving languages from extinction matters for the discipline of linguistics in the same way that preserving manuscripts matters for the study of literature. And second, in the other direction, language extinction lends linguistics a new importance: only through the skills that linguistics develops can anyone come to understand the structure of a previously unstudied or undescribed language, and thus ensure that an understanding of its properties will not be forever lost to humanity.

And for a plethora of reasons it is vital that we should have a detailed, objective, scientific understanding of the languages of the world – all of them, whether well-studied and thriving among hundreds of millions of users or known only to tiny communities.

### *Languages and the Puzzle of Acquisition*

Languages are not all cut to the same pattern. They are wildly diverse, displaying huge differences in a number of different aspects that have to be studied in rather different ways. To be specific, we have to distinguish:

- phonetics (the production, perception, and acoustic nature of speech sounds);

- phonology (the systems of sounds in particular languages – some languages use barely a dozen consonants and vowels while others use hundreds);
- morphology (the structure of words – some languages use sequences of simple one-syllable words while others build up words of complex structure and meaning);
- syntax (the ways words are combined into phrases and sentences – morphology and syntax are often lumped together as grammar);
- semantics (the systematic expression of literal meanings); and
- pragmatics (the conveying of meaning by uttering sentences in specific contexts).

Let me cite just one example of diversity from syntax. To a speaker of English or French, it seems natural, even obvious and inevitable, that if you're going to give a simple characterization of the diet of baleen whales in three words, you would first name the active participant (whales), then what they are claimed to do (eat), and then what they are said to do it to (krill): you'd say *Whales eat krill*. So you use the order Subject–Verb–Object (SVO). You might even think that was built into our brains as the way to organize things (some French philosophers definitely thought that in the eighteenth century). But research in syntax has steadily undercut any such view.

To begin with, in thousands of languages such as Japanese, Mongolian, Hindi, and Turkish the verb is normally at the end of the clause: they use SOV order as a default. The SOV languages form a larger percentage of the total than the SVO languages.

And hundreds of other languages (examples include Irish, Hawaiian, and Classical Arabic) typically use the order VSO.

That still leaves the possibility that every human language favours having the subject before the object. But that is not true either. In Malagasy (of Madagascar) and many other Austronesian languages, and in Tzotzil (Mexico) and many other Mayan languages, the usual order is VOS.

Could there also be languages where the default order in the clause has the object first? In 1976, I believed the answer was no. Several candidates had been suggested, but I found it easy to show that they had been misdiagnosed. I said so in a lecture course I was teaching at University College London, and a middle-aged man who had recently been taken on as a PhD student raised his hand and said he thought he knew of a language that favoured OVS. I told him that almost certainly it was an SOV language in which the subject was sometimes postponed for stylistic reasons, but we'd talk about it later. We did. And he convinced me that he was right and I was wrong.

The PhD student was Desmond Derbyshire. As a young man, an accountant from Darlington visiting missionary friends in Guyana, he had once got completely lost in the tropical forest during an ill-advised short walk on his own. During his night alone in the forest he prayed, and made a promise to God that if he could survive this he would dedicate his life to being a missionary and Bible translator like his friends. He could have been attacked and eaten by a jaguar, but he wasn't. In the morning he managed to find a river, and was soon rescued (rivers are like main roads in the jungles of South America).

He kept his private promise, trained with the Summer Institute of Linguistics as a missionary linguist, signed up with the Wycliffe Bible Translators, and was sent to work in a village where a group of Brazilian Indians (numbering little more than a hundred) spoke a language called Hixkaryana, about which hardly anything was known to linguists. Long before I met him he had learned it well, decided on an alphabet for it, and translated the entire New Testament into it with the help of native speakers. So we were actually able to examine his translation as evidence. Sure enough, 100% of the transitive clauses (those with a verb that takes an object) were OVS. The same was true in stories and memoirs by native speakers that he had recorded and transcribed. The word for 'jaguar' in Hixkaryana is *kamara*; 'ate' or 'used to eat' is *yonoye*; and 'person' or 'people' is *toto*; but the translation of 'Jaguars used to eat people' is *Toto yonoye kamara*.

Derbyshire, who was to become one of the finest scholars I ever knew, wrote his PhD thesis on the syntax of Hixkaryana and its closest relatives. Together we contacted other missionaries in South America and researched forgotten anthropological literature, and we found evidence of a dozen or more OVS languages, and even identified a couple of OSV languages. It was a complete surprise to me, and a refutation of my publicly announced beliefs at the time, but that is how science progresses: by stating clearly what I thought was true I had triggered Derbyshire's realization that his long years of work in the Brazilian jungle had come up with something theoretically noteworthy; and by welcoming evidence that my beliefs could be wrong I had been able to participate in discovering something quite new. We had established that all six of the logically possible orders of subject, object, and verb occur in at least some languages as the normal, standard order. The notion that all humans naturally think in SVO now looks thoroughly implausible.

Such discoveries have posed a scientific puzzle: how human languages can be so strikingly diverse worldwide yet so readily learned by young children. Human infants are certainly born pre-equipped for the task in some way that is not paralleled by the young of any other species; but how their innate abilities relate to the acquisition of specific languages remains a crucial unsolved problem.

To work on that problem we need explicit descriptions of as many languages as possible. Identify the speech sounds used in a language; find out how they are deployed in the pronunciation patterns of the language; decide on a way in which its utterances can be unambiguously transcribed (thousands of the languages of the world have no tradition of being written down, hence no alphabet); determine the words and their meanings and internal structures; work out what the principles are whereby words can be combined into phrases and sentences; and elucidate the systematic ways in which those sentences are associated with meanings. To accomplish all this for a language, even quite superficially, takes not months but years. Derbyshire worked on Hixkaryana for more than three decades. Thousands of scholars have worked on languages like Greek, Latin, and English for centuries, and still new discoveries are being made all the time.

Describing the languages of the world, and developing a theoretical understanding of how they work and how they are acquired by infants, is fundamental scientific research, not just routine cataloguing. But it has potential applications of great practical importance, as I will explain in parts of the rest of this book.

# 2

# How Sentences Work

'Words have consequences', says Sir Harold Evans in his book *Do I Make Myself Clear?* People often say that, as if words on their own could have effects or do things to us. But it's not a defensible claim. Think about it: what consequences does *incomparability* have? Or *magnify*? Or *despite*?

People talk as if it was words doing the work – indeed, they often seem to conceive of languages as nothing more or less than big bags of words – but in truth the consequences of any use of language follow from the utterance, in specific contexts, of more complex entities called sentences. Those are formed by arranging various words in particular ways. Knowing the words of a language but not the phonology or grammar would be almost useless. In fact the specific words employed in a sentence matter relatively little. Someone who says *Bring me my faithful dog* could easily have said it in a way that doesn't share a single word with that utterance: *Fetch that trusty hound of mine.*

The most you could really say about words is that the choice of one word rather than another in a sentence can have consequences when the sentence is used in a certain context. But the key to what separates the cognitive powers of humans from those of all other creatures lies in the principles of syntax (sentence structure), semantics (literal meaning of sentences), and pragmatics (conveyance of utterance meaning in context). Investigating those principles is a fascinating, difficult, and important task, forming a core subpart of theoretical linguistics. This chapter is concerned with the part of it that has traditionally, for some 2,000 years, been known as grammar.

### Grammar and Grammatophobia

It's odd how the very mention of grammar can provoke strongly negative feelings of nervousness or hostility in nonlinguists. Draw someone's attention to the structure of the bones in their hands and it doesn't trouble them much; but any mention of the structure of the sentences they use makes them edgy, as if they're being criticized. Something has obviously gone awry with the public presentation of linguistic science.

I should note at this point that linguists use the word 'grammar' in at least two ways: (i) to refer to the structural properties and organization that the sentences in a given language have, and (ii) to refer to a description of those properties worked out by a linguist.

The ambiguity is rarely pernicious. Sometimes I'll talk about 'the grammar of English', meaning the structure that English sentences actually have – the structure that grammarians are attempting to reveal and explicitly describe when they say things like that English uses SVO order as the default. In that sense English has always had grammar and always will. It changes slowly over centuries (a thousand years ago English was mostly SOV), but that merely means that the structure evolves. The point is that it can't be regarded as good or bad at any given stage; it's just the way it is.

But sometimes instead I will talk about devising or writing 'a grammar of English': a description or theory of the structure inherent in the sentences of the language. In that sense, there was no such thing as an English grammar in the year 1400: nobody seems to have tried to write one until 1586, when a printer named William Bullokar published an initial attempt, closely following the model set by the grammar of Latin published by William Lily earlier that century (the first one written in English). Bullokar was trying to set down an account of the principles that define English sentences as opposed to those of Latin or any other language. Such an enterprise can be executed well or poorly: in that sense, some grammars are good, and some are not.

The statements made in English grammars are in fact often mistaken where they disagree with the habitual practices of English speakers. Nonlinguists seem to assume that rules of grammar are stipulated by godlike authorities who are not to be questioned. They also seem to think that the rules comprise a fairly short list of simple edicts that you can find in books somewhere: maxims saying always do $x$ or never do $y$. And they believe these rules are mostly ignored in everyday conversation. In other words, people see grammar as analogous to the regulative instructions and warnings you find in the user's guide leaflet when you unpack a new chainsaw: 'Remove scabbard before use'; 'Keep chain well lubricated'; 'Always wear safety goggles'; 'Do not touch chain while motor is running'; 'Do not stand directly beneath the branch you are cutting'; that sort of thing. Only without the personal safety motivation. No wonder they think grammar is boring and pointless.

Educated people generally have dim memories of being taught some of these rules, but their recollection is often pretty shaky. There's something bad about ending a sentence with a preposition, or beginning it with a conjunction; there are places where you shouldn't say *me* and places where you ought to say *whom* . . . And pretty soon they can't tell you much more.

Tangled up with these half-forgotten memories of scraps of grammar teaching are evident feelings of unease. When I make the mistake of telling some stranger that my academic work includes research on the grammar of English, they tend to say, 'Oh, my grammar is awful', or 'Ooh, I'd better watch what I say then!' – as if I'm about to start picking on them for the way they speak, or I'm bound to look down on them for it. This kind of low linguistic self-esteem is a sad consequence of unsuccessful teaching about language. Bad English teachers may try to bully their students into changing the variety of English they have grown up speaking, but linguists don't. Some speakers of English follow slightly different rules from others, but linguists don't see that as entitling anyone to accuse others of being 'wrong' in the way they speak.

I often try to point out that (for example) ornithologists aren't judgemental about birds: they don't condemn penguins as too lazy to fly. And in the same way, linguistic scientists don't take a harsh view of the French for wantonly putting adjectives after the noun (*vin <u>blanc</u>*) instead of before (*<u>white</u> wine*). So linguists won't judge your worth on the basis of whether you say *if I were you* or *if I was you* (both of which are widely used).

The trouble with making points of this sort is that it is regularly misinterpreted as a sign of relaxing constraints and lowering standards. I get accused of thinking that 'anything goes provided you make yourself understood'. I don't believe anything of the sort. I believe it's the responsibility of linguists not to condemn what they see and hear but to frame their descriptions of English (or whatever language) in a way that captures the regularities that its fluent speakers typically employ when structuring their sentences.

It is amazingly hard to get people to see that the linguist is interested in **ascertaining what the actual grammatical constraints of the given language are.** When a linguist says it's 'grammatical' to begin a paragraph with a coordinator (a word like *and*, *or*, *but*, or *nor*, also known as 'conjunctions'), they don't mean that it infringes a rule but they'll let you off with a warning this time, like a police officer who caught you driving at 34 m.p.h. in a 30 m.p.h. street. They mean it doesn't infringe any rule that belongs in an accurate grammar of English at all.

English teachers may have reasons for encouraging students to try writing sentences that don't begin with *and* (to get them to experiment with new ways of joining sentences together, perhaps), but they shouldn't say that there is a rule against it, because that just isn't true. The evidence for this is overwhelming. The right rules are the ones that experienced users of the language follow (setting aside the occasional cases of accidental slips that the users themselves would regard as not having been their intent).

So what would you regard as an example of writing by an experienced user? Was Sir Arthur Conan Doyle experienced enough? The eleventh sentence in *The Hound of the Baskervilles* begins with *but* and number twenty begins with *and*. How about H.G. Wells? The eighth sentence in *The War of the Worlds* begins with *and*. If you'd like to see a thousand such factual observations drawn from famous and excellent literature, I could have a report ready by lunchtime.

The point I'm making is that we can study the evidence of expert use of the language to figure out what the correct rules are. It's not the other way round – we don't figure out who the expert users are by reference to how closely they adhere to whatever beliefs about the rules have been handed down to us from the eighteenth century.

American linguists during the twentieth century made a concerted effort to change ideas about how to study grammar. Many had been informed by perspective-altering observations made while studying American Indian languages, and it inspired them to try to look at English as if through new eyes. They rebutted old myths, discovered new generalizations, and realized that much standard English grammar teaching was scarcely worth having: the books purporting to state the rules simply didn't capture the actual structure of the language. Sadly, their work has so far had hardly any impact on the general public's understanding.

### *Why Most Grammars Are Wrong*

Claims about the grammar of a language can be wrong in three different ways: (i) because the language has changed, (ii) because prejudice has clouded perceptions of what the facts are, or (iii) because of analytical blunders that obscure the description of the facts.

It is always possible to make generalizations that are overtaken by events, of course, but in fact (i) is much less significant than (ii) or (iii). Many seem to believe otherwise: when I mention to nonlinguists that working on English grammar involves deep and difficult problems, people very often say, 'Oh yes, well, it's changing all the time, isn't it?' – as if the trouble had to do with describing something that was in flux. Language is indeed changing and evolving all the time, but the process is extremely slow. Even over a century, the changes in grammar that English undergoes are quite trivial. Teenage vampire fans can still read the original text of *Dracula*, published a century before they were born.

Type (ii) errors involve preferences, prejudices, peeves, and pieties. Personal likes and dislikes, or idiosyncratic reformist yearnings, may warp the work of a grammar-writer, interfering with the business of giving an accurate account about the actual structure of the language. A shockingly high proportion of highly educated English speakers believe in fictive rules that would forbid prepositions at ends of clauses (*What are you afraid of?*), *they* with singular antecedents (*Everyone should bring their own lunch*), plural agreement with *none* (*None of us are perfect*), and all sorts of other familiar usages occurring in literary as well as conversational English.

Type (iii) is a bit harder to spot. Grammarians can do the analysis wrong even while getting the data right. For centuries grammars have been repeating generalizations that simply don't work, or grouping things together when they don't belong together.

They state that a noun is by definition the name of a person, place, or thing. How can that be true, when *emptiness* is a noun?

They define an adjective as a word that modifies a noun, telling you what kind of thing it names. But in *tree surgeon* the word *tree* tells you what kind of surgeon it is, yet *tree* is the name of a thing, so by the previous definition it has to be a noun.

They say that the subject of a sentence is 'the doer of the action'; but in what sense does *it* refer to the doer of an action in a sentence like *It's no use complaining*?

They inform us that the object in a sentence is the noun identifying the entity that 'receives the action'; but how does that odd phrase apply to *The building is undergoing renovation*?

They assert that prepositions stand before nouns and relate them to other nouns. But that means *up* is a preposition in *The flag went up the flagpole* but not in *The flag went up*. Surely it has the same function in each case, of indicating the direction of travel.

They treat *he cried* as a 'noun clause' in *They say he cried* but an 'adverb clause' in *It was so sad he cried*; but surely these are just two different roles a clause can have, not two kinds of clause.

And so on for page after page of ill-considered dogma that has been repeated (indeed, plagiarized) from grammar book to grammar book for three centuries.

It is embarrassing to compare the progress in understanding English syntax with developments in palaeontology. Major discoveries of fossilized dinosaur skeletons began around 1800. Initial mis-analysis led to their being interpreted as the bones of big stupid lizards that became extinct because mammals outsmarted them. Two centuries of progress in scientific palaeontology subsequently revealed that dinosaurs were of all sizes, and were almost certainly endothermic (warm-blooded) and fairly intelligent creatures, in many cases active and energetic. They dominated the earth for hundreds of millions of years, and far from perishing at the end of the Cretaceous, have billions of living descendants now known as birds. Dinosaur zoology has been utterly revolutionized.

But during the same century English grammar stood still, despite the fact that evidence was so much easier to access (comparing sentences is a lot easier than extracting allosaurus vertebrae from a bone bed in Utah). Grammar books for school students and the general public spent the nineteenth century simply repeating dogma from the age of George III. In the twentieth century linguistics began to achieve a huge expansion in our understanding of the principles of English sentence construction, and illuminated the structure of hundreds of other languages, but very few members of the general public know anything about that, and grammar books from the nineteenth century remain in print. The important task that remains is to connect modern linguistic insights to the production of grammars and dictionaries.

Sadly, the educational testing industry has in many cases constructed tests based on spurious grammar rules that purists have exaggerated or simply invented. The hapless test-takers are required to identify alleged errors in perfectly grammatical sentences. Until recent reforms this was true of the Scholastic Aptitude Test or SAT used to assess the suitability of American students for college or university entrance. It remains true of English language teaching in many countries. The cruel, time-wasting nonsense of training students to condemn certain familiar patterns as 'wrong' because of superstitions from earlier centuries is a terrible way to teach language, and should long since have been abandoned everywhere, but is in fact commonplace around the world.


## *The Five-Million-Dollar Grammar Slip*

You might think that the details of grammatical rules, however intricate or difficult to figure out they might be, can't possibly have much practical importance. But that's not so. At least, not if you think five million dollars counts as important, as a dairy company recently found out in court

A 1995 minimum-wage law in Maine mandated time-and-a-half pay for required work beyond forty hours per week, except in certain job categories. One category of exceptions covered jobs involving perishable foodstuffs, and specifically the 'canning, processing, preserving, freezing, drying, marketing, storing, packing for shipment or distribution' of perishables. But wait a minute: is that eight categories, the last one being 'packing for shipment or distribution'? Or is it nine, the eighth being 'packing for shipment' and the ninth, 'distribution'? (See Table 1.) Five drivers for the Oakhurst Dairy decided that the eight-category interpretation was the one the lawmakers had intended, and since

**Table 1**

| Eight categories: | | Nine categories: | |
|---|---|---|---|
| 1 | canning | 1 | canning |
| 2 | processing | 2 | processing |
| 3 | preserving | 3 | preserving |
| 4 | freezing | 4 | freezing |
| 5 | drying | 5 | drying |
| 6 | marketing | 6 | marketing |
| 7 | storing | 7 | storing |
| 8 | packing for shipment or distribution | 8 | packing for shipment |
| | | 9 | distribution |

'packing for shipment or distribution' is not their job, they did not fall under the exception and were entitled to overtime pay when asked to work more than forty hours a week. They had not been receiving overtime pay, so they brought a class action suit against the dairy on behalf of all 127 drivers. Oakhurst Dairy maintained, unsurprisingly, that the nine-category interpretation was the correct one. By March 2017 the issue was under consideration by the United States Court of Appeals for the First Circuit.

All that the Oakhurst interpretation has to assume about the grammar of the relevant statute is that although the legislators could have made themselves completely clear by putting a comma after *packing for shipment*, they chose not to. That is entirely plausible. In a coordinate structure

– an expression formed with a coordinator such as *or* – a comma before the sole coordinator is known as the 'serial comma'. Some writers use it and others don't. And in fact the court laws in Maine always omit the serial comma: this practice is stipulated in pages 113–14 of the *Maine Legislative Drafting Manual* (which is available to everyone online).

Under the drivers' view, you have to assume something much less plausible: that the legislators left out a crucial word. Coordinators (words like *and*, *or*, *but*, and *nor*) serve to link the items in a syndetic coordination such as *Norway, Sweden, Denmark, and Finland*. Under the eight-category view the crucial coordination is lacking a coordinator. It says:

> *canning, processing, preserving, freezing, drying, marketing, storing, packing for shipment or distribution*

If *packing for shipment or distribution* is just one item, then there is no coordinator linking the eight items in the whole phrase (there should be an *or* after *storing*).

Now, such constructions do occur. They are known as asyndetic coordinations. They have either an *and* meaning (as in the obvious interpretation of *We can't make a Waldorf salad; we'd need celery, apples, walnuts, grapes*) or an *or* meaning (as in the obvious interpretation of *What if there were a fire, a flood, an earthquake?*). So it's not that asyndetic coordinations are incorrect; they're just inexplicit about the *and/or* difference. Inexplicitness of that sort would be very risky in stating a law, and is hardly ever found. (Notice, if we took the supposed eight job categories to be linked with an implicit *and*, then nobody would ever be covered by the exception, because no single person has a job involving canning, processing, preserving, freezing, drying, marketing, storing, **and** packing for shipment or distribution.)

Arguments about purely linguistic points of this sort went back and forth between the two sides' lawyers, and the court struggled to arrive at a clear view of what the statute had meant. What they ultimately decided was that they simply could not determine the intent of the statute. So they turned to a different principle altogether. Labour law is intended to protect workers rather than bosses, they noted, so doubts about the interpretation of a clause should always be resolved in favour of the workers. They ruled that the drivers should have been receiving overtime pay. In February 2018 Oakhurst settled the case by agreeing to give the drivers $5 million in back pay.

Ironically, the state legislature had meanwhile returned to the drafting of the law to clarify it. The revised version makes it clear that drivers of distribution vehicles are **not** included in the exception, and thus are not eligible for the overtime rate. As if determined to make the separate categories more explicit without violating the instructions of the *Maine Legislative Drafting Manual*, they upgrade the commas to semicolons, and write:

> *canning; processing; preserving; freezing; drying; marketing; storing; packing for shipment; or distribution*

Under the rewritten law, it is clear that they have written a syndetic *or* coordination (and the semicolons ensure that they do not violate the legislative drafting manual!). So the drivers are once again **not** entitled to time and a half for required overtime.

Notice that the relevant arguments don't turn on anybody's grammar being 'bad' or 'good'. What's crucial is what the actual principles of sentence construction are, and how a given meaning can be unambiguously expressed. The relevant issues may seem to involve tiny yet head-swirlingly difficult details. But in fact they only involve the clues to structure and meaning that we use all the time to understand what we've read or what people say to us. Students of linguistics are simply more used to looking at those clues to structure and meaning, and codifying them explicitly. Linguists have well-tried tests for figuring out what the principles of English syntax are, and thus what meaning a given form of words will bear under the usual principles. The work of the appeals court in the Oakhurst case was strikingly analogous to the work of linguists trying to identify and make precise the rules of a language.

The need for collaboration between lawyers and linguists is not as widely appreciated as it should be. And the advisability of linguists being involved in the work of legislatures drafting laws is even less appreciated. When a full-scale court battle has erupted over the syntax and semantics of a sentence in some law or contract, it's already way too late.

The computational linguist Jason Eisner pointed out that the reasoning needed in thinking about the case involved a point in the logic of probability known as Bayes' theorem, which basically says that the probability of a guess being right given some evidence for its truth is proportional to the probability that the evidence would look like that if the guess were correct. The court needed to consider not just 'How likely is it that the legislators meant *x*, given that they wrote *y*?' but also 'How likely is it that the legislators would have written *y*, if their intent was to express *x*?' Bayes' theorem assures us that the two degrees of probability are tightly linked and proportionate.

The same reasoning applies much more generally to linguists trying to write a grammar: they have to keep in mind not just 'How likely is it that the grammar rule *R* is correct, given that we find *E* as the evidence of how people speak and write?' but also that the answer will be proportional to the answer to a different question: 'How likely is it that the evidence would look like *E* if the correct grammar had rule *R*?' That enables us to glean statistical evidence for the existence of negative conditions. Consider the fact that we hear phrases like *eat the pizza up*, and *eat up the pizza*, and *eat it up*, but never \**eat up it*. (Linguists write an asterisk before a string of words to indicate that it is not grammatically correct.) How probable is it that \**eat up it* would never occur if it were grammatically allowable? Highly improbable. Its failure to occur signals that a grammatical restriction probably forbids it. Suppose that (perhaps for evolution-related reasons) we're subconsciously and involuntarily sensitive to any mismatch between 'never shows up' and 'should have shown up by now'. That built-in sensitivity might be one of the factors making language acquisition possible.

# 3

# Words, Meaning, and Thought

At hundreds of sites on the web you can find lists of allegedly 'untranslatable words' (heavily plagiarized from each other) that are often shared via emails and social media. And there is something about them that seems very odd when you stop to think about it: they all come with translations for each word!

A list of truly untranslatable words would not attract much readership or sharing. If *mugugabamanka* really has no translation (and it doesn't, because I made it up), there's nothing interesting to say about it. What seems to appeal to people about the supposedly untranslatable words is not that English cannot express what they mean, but the property of having a rich and evocative sense that calls for several lines to capture it in English. These words don't lack a translation; they lack a translation that is both perfectly accurate and exactly one word long. That's a very different matter.

The Danish word *hyggelig* often figures in such lists. One explains its meaning by saying that it 'refers to a warm, friendly, cosy, delightfully intimate moment or thing' and 'gives off imagery of a candlelit winter evening at home with warm blankets and maybe a bit of alcohol'. So 'cosiness' does most of the work of translating it, and 'warm, friendly, and intimate cosiness' does almost perfectly; but people say that until you've spent a winter snuggled up with loved ones in front of a fire in a farmhouse in Denmark you won't quite experience the feeling that it typically evokes in Danes.

Calling this untranslatability stretches the linguistic notion of translation beyond recognition. What's failing to carry over has to do with experience, culture, and first-hand involvement in practices. And that raises a crucial point about how linguistics contributes to clarification about the relation of language to thought. It is not that linguistics sorts out all the issues and answers all the questions: these matters are deep, complex, and ill-understood, and call for work in philosophy, psychology, and neuroscience. But some elementary linguistics can clarify our grasp of the crucial notion of meaning, and clear away some of the more confused assumptions people have about language and thought.

## *Varieties of Meaning*

Most people who find lists of untranslatable words interesting and charming are implicitly collapsing several different notions of word meaning. Semanticists – linguists who work specifically on linguistic meaning – are very used to the business of separating these out.

Words have ranges of literal applicability that determine their contributions to the minimal meanings of the sentences containing them. This is clearest with scientifically defined terms (things are very different with other kinds of word, as we'll see). *Monotreme* denotes the mammals in the Monotremata order including platypuses and echidnas; and *oviparous* denotes the property of reproducing by depositing unhatched eggs outside the body. So *Monotremes are oviparous* states that the animals of the Monotremata order lay eggs.

It isn't always that straightforward, because some words have components of their meaning that make a clear meaning contribution without affecting truth conditions. Take *but*, as used to join sentences: *Harald is a Swede but he doesn't speak Swedish* is true precisely when *Harald is a Swede and he doesn't speak Swedish* is true, and vice versa. If one is true (or false), the other is as well. Yet clearly the meanings differ. The one with *but* seems to imply that given the first part (that Harald is a Swede) you would be inclined to believe that he speaks Swedish, and the utterer wants to head you off at the pass to prepare you for the second part, which contradicts that natural belief. *But* contributes an important component of the main meaning of the sentence that is not captured by truth conditions.

There are also cases of metaphorical use. *Wooden* denotes the property of being made of wood, but if I describe a lecturer's style of delivery as wooden, I don't mean it's composed of fibrous tissue from the non-leafy parts of trees; I'm using a kind of shortcut to give you a sense of the style: not supple or responsive, not engaging or entertaining . . . you know what wood is like, so analogize.

Next, there are curiously peripheral implications associated with some words, allowing them to carry a secondary message, not connected to its denotation. If I say 'I've lost my damn keys', *damn* doesn't convey any property of my keys. That is, *my damn keys* has exactly the same denotation as *my keys*. What *damn* conveys, as an undeniable part of its meaning (linguists call it a conventional implicature), is an indication that I'm annoyed at the situation expressed in the main content of what I've said. If I said 'I've lost my damn keys and I'm entirely happy and relaxed about that', I'd be both expressing irritation and denying that I was, in the same breath.

One further kind of word meaning, perhaps the most relevant to the lists of untranslatable words we began with, are the miscellaneous overtones and associations that many words have. Medieval logicians called these connotations. Take the words *small* and *little*. They both denote the property of coming lower on the scale of size relative to some suitable context-dependent standard. (The standard is relative: a small elephant is far bigger than a huge mouse. But that's not the important issue here.) The connotational difference is that while using *small* seems to focus on an actual size measurement, choosing *little* seems to carry a connotation of something like cuteness.

So the phrase *a small aircraft carrier* would be a perfectly normal description for a ship that, though still huge (as aircraft carriers have to be), is small compared to the average for that class of ships. But *a little aircraft carrier* doesn't sound the same at all. It talks of the ship as if it were a toy.

And although it would be natural to describe a gift as *a lovely little brooch*, to call it *a lovely small brooch* would seem to contrast small brooches with more generously proportioned ones, which rather undercuts the praise.

Vast numbers of everyday words carry connotations of this sort and many other kinds:

- *Gypsy* denotes a person of Romany heritage in a relatively neutral way, whereas *Gyppo* denotes the same ethnic group but is regarded as insulting;
- *rabbit* denotes a species of animal in the Leporidae family, whereas *bunny* is a name for the same kind of animal that is more suitable for use in talking with a child;
- *thinking* is an ordinary word for silent cognitive activity, while *ratiocination* is a much more learned-sounding word referring to exactly the same activity;
- *quarrel* denotes a difference of opinion with some kind of emotional content, best sorted out by having the parties calm down and get back on better terms, while *dispute* suggests something more serious and objective, perhaps calling for arbitration.

In addition to the five different kinds of word meaning I've now reviewed, extra meaning, beyond anything in the words, can be implied in a given context in a way that has an interesting deniability. Suppose I say: *I noticed you had a letter from the doctor.* That might very easily suggest that I'd like to know what the letter said. (Why else would I mention it? Surely I'm not just commenting on how observant I am about the post on the doormat.) Yet the suggestion is entirely cancellable. If you say, 'Do you want to read it?', but you seem a bit annoyed, I could answer, 'No, not at all, it's your private business.' I haven't thereby rescinded anything I actually said.

Suggested meanings of this sort are known to linguists as conversational implicatures, and it can be extremely important to understand how they work. A perjury conviction cannot be based on a conversational implicature: you only commit perjury if the denotational meaning of something you said under oath was false and you knew it. Misleading the court with a conversational implicature may be morally disreputable, but it can't make you guilty of perjury. In defamation law, on the other hand, things are completely different: libel lawyers have a special term for conversational implicatures: they call them 'innuendoes', and you can be successfully sued for libel over an innuendo. By saying 'I doubt whether tea is Jones's favourite tipple' and thus inducing people to have a belief that Jones is a drunkard, you have defamed him, and he can sue.

All of the half-dozen kinds of meaning create difficulties for translatability. Conversational implicatures are perhaps the trickiest because they depend on people's everyday knowledge and common sense.

Armed with just this tiny introduction to the rich and complex subdisciplines of semantics and pragmatics, we can return to the issue of those untranslatable words and their translations, and make things a bit clearer.

First, it's absolutely clear that you cannot always expect a single word in some other language to have a literal equivalent in English that is also a single word, not even if you just consider denotational meaning. *Schnitzel* in German is certainly translatable, but 'breaded veal chop' is about as short a translation as you can find, so one German word takes three in English. There will be English words that take three words to translate into German as well (I'll leave finding a few as an exercise for the reader). But that doesn't preclude excellent translations.

The second point is that to demand translation equivalents that share all the same other aspects of meaning – non-denotational meaning, implicatures, connotations – would be to make translation infeasible. All sorts of obvious literal translation equivalents will fail to have exactly the same connotations. Nobody cites *garçon* in French as untranslatable, despite the fact that in French it sometimes means 'waiter', which English 'boy' never does, and English *boy* was used in past decades as a highly insulting form of address by whites speaking to blacks in the southern states of the USA, which *garçon* never was. None of this makes *garçon* untranslatable: *The boy is here* is a fine English translation of *Le garçon est ici*.

The claim of impossibility implicit in the lists of 'untranslatable' words pushes the idea of translation to an unreasonable extreme. Being able to understand things said in a foreign language shouldn't be taken to entail being able to merge with the consciousness of its speakers, and access all the connections present in their entire network of subjective experiences and memories, as in the Vulcan mind-melding of *Star Trek*.

## *Many Words for Snow?*

The appeal of allegedly untranslatable words is closely linked to people's fascination with the two-part idea that (i) languages differ in the range of different concepts they have words for, and (ii) the concepts that their users can form and think about are limited by their language. The main pleasure of learning a new foreign language is often said to be that you get an introduction to a new culture in which entirely new concepts are added to your way of seeing the world. And hundreds of writers have claimed that 'Eskimos' (the Yupik and Inuit peoples of the Arctic) have several, or dozens, or scores of different words for snow, giving them a view of the world completely different from that of an English speaker.

A paper by Laura Martin at an anthropology conference in 1982 pointed out something odd about this claim about 'the Eskimos': although there was a 1911 source in which an anthropologist with first-hand knowledge had mentioned four different snow-related words in an Eskimoan language of Canada, sources of later date exaggerated this number and embellished the claim. The example had appeared over and over again, in everything from psychology textbooks to newspaper articles, and with each repetition the numbers were tending to get bigger and bigger.

Professor Martin had a long battle getting her paper into print. Journal reviewers hated it, perhaps because the people whose behaviour was under examination were social scientists like them. But a shortened version did finally appear in the journal *American Anthropologist* in 1986, and in 1989 I publicized it in a humorous article aimed at linguists. I mocked the exaggerations, and cited additional examples of them. From magazine articles to management courses, people were eagerly spreading the baseless story that 'the Eskimos' had twenty or forty-three or a hundred words for snow, without ever giving any evidence or examples. Dictionaries of Eskimoan languages do exist, but they were never cited. And the apparently random numbers people gave were getting larger and larger over the years.

I called my article 'The Great Eskimo Vocabulary Hoax', deliberately stretching the term 'hoax' to suggest that our entire culture was hoaxing itself. It might have been better to call it a meme consisting of a large class of highly similar factoids citing different numbers. Writers seemed to be popping it into their articles just for something to say. You'd find an article in a travel magazine on, say, the coffee shops of Vienna, and the author would begin: 'It is said that the Eskimos have 150 words for snow, and the Viennese must surely have at least that many for cakes and pastries . . .' It doesn't need to be a true claim about Eskimoan languages to serve its purpose here, it's just a thing people say (because other people have said it). But over time I think people may have started to assume it is true on the grounds that everyone says it.

Even in university textbooks and courses, the factoid about Eskimoan snow vocabulary size is served up to students without any underlying data – and also without any clear conception of why it would be interesting if it were true. Would you really start seeing snow differently if you were taught many different words for different types of it? Possibly; but surely that would be because you were learning about the varieties of snow phenomena, not because of the words.

And would you naturally invent lots of different words for something if you lived surrounded by it and it was crucial to your life? There's a nice joke about this, in which two young fish swimming along encounter an older and more experienced fish swimming the other way who greets them and comments on how nice the water is this morning. The two younger fish swim on silently for a while, and then one of them says, 'What the hell is water?'

Just because something is all around you and essential to your existence, that doesn't in any way suggest that you'll have a plethora of names for it.

We only have one word for air, except that we call it 'wind' or a 'breeze' when it moves detectably.

The importance of linguistics here is that it can contribute factually based description, and perhaps some kind of basis for potential theories of how vocabulary size might relate to concept formation. So, what are the facts?

Briefly, all the Eskimoan languages seem to have a noun spelled *qanik* that means 'snowflake', and in nearly all of them there is a different word beginning *aput* meaning 'snow covering the ground'. Beyond that, you can find a few more clearly snow-related words with meanings like 'blizzard', 'snowdrift', 'new snowfall', and so on (it's never clear what exactly to count), but not very many. Not much more than in English (*snow*, *slush*, *sleet*, *blizzard*, *drift*, *whiteout*, *powder*. . .).

And closer analysis reveals that some of the words that have occasionally been given as examples of snow words (by the very few people who have tried to make lists of them) are not really snow words at all. For example, West Greenlandic Inuit *illuksaq* has been cited as a word meaning 'snow of the type you can build igloos with'; but -*ksaq* means 'stuff for making', and *illu* (in Canadian Inuktitut *iglu*) means 'house' (that's the source of English *igloo*), so *illuksaq* just means 'house-building materials'.

That would include snow firm enough to cut into blocks to build an igloo, but could also include plywood and corrugated iron. It's not a snow word, it's a construction-material word.

Mentioning the suffixal element -*ksaq* touches on a truly fascinating fact about Eskimoan languages, which has nothing inherently to do with snow yet in a sense kicks the number of snow words up to arbitrarily huge numbers. Eskimoan languages allow new words to be built by adding meaningful units called postbases and then putting inflectional suffixes on the result, to a degree that boggles the mind. You can make up new complex snow words until the seals come home using just a small number of basic roots plus a series of postbases. That makes it effectively pointless trying to count the number of words: there are as many as you could possibly want. Millions of words for snow, but also millions of words for fish or clouds or blood or anything else.

Let's look briefly at how a fairly lengthy complex word is built up in the Western dialect of Greenlandic Inuit, known in Greenland (Kalaallit Nunaat) as Kalaallisut. We'll build up a huge word (a verb) with a crazy sentence-like meaning. I've deliberately made it crazy in order to show it's not just a one-off dictionary oddity like the artificially invented English word *floccinaucinihilipilification*.

# Words, Meaning, and Thought

We'll start with a root meaning 'fish'. As we go through the following steps you'll notice that final consonants of words sometimes change when you add a postbase or an inflectional suffix.

*aalisagaq* 'fish'

*aalisagaq* + *oq* = *aalisagakoq* 'fish remains'

*aalisagakoq* + *sunni-* = *aalisagakorsunni-* 'smell of fish remains'

*aalisagakorsunni* + *k-* = *aalisagakorsunnik-* 'to smell of fish remains'

*aalisagakorsunnik* + *toq* = *aalisagakorsunnittoq* 'something that smells of fish remains'

*aalisagakorsunnittoq* + *sior* = *aalisagakorsunnittorsior* 'to look for something that smells of fish remains'

*aalisagakorsunnittorsior* + *iartor-* = *aalisagakorsunnittorsioriartor* 'to go out to look for something that smells of fish remains'

*aalisagakorsunnittorsioriartor* + *put* = *aalisagakorsunnittorsioriartorput* 'they went out to look for something that smells like fish remains'

That's a very complex idea to be able to express in one word. But amazingly, it can be further lengthened. There is an element spelled *-ngooq* that when suffixed to any Kalaallisut verb adds an implication that the clause is only reporting hearsay, not eyewitness testimony. (It's a common feature in languages of many different families to have a 'hearsay' marker of this sort.) So we can do this:

*aalisagakorsunnittorsioriartorput* + *ngooq* = *aalisa-gakorsunnittorsioriartorpunngooq* 'It is said that they went out to look for something that smells of fish remains'

And even that does not hit any upper limit on length or complexity (there really isn't such a limit). Adding *-aasiit* to the verb of a clause contributes the information that it is reporting something broadly in line with what you would have expected to be true. So we have:

*aalisagakorsunnittorsioriartorpunngooq* + *aasiit* =*aalisagakorsunnittorsioriartorpunngooraasiit* 'As might be expected, it is said that they went out to look for something that smells of fish remains'

Very few languages in the world allow word-building of this extreme sort. The Eskimoan languages are indeed extraordinary. But it's not some large inventory of roots denoting specific types of snow that makes Kalaallisut amazing to a linguist. Of course, if it were true, that would not be all that surprising. (I wish I could have used *-aasiit* when saying that!) After all, printers who deal with fonts all day have lots of words for fonts. But the claim about snow words just doesn't seem to be true. If there's one respect in which the minds of Eskimoan speakers work in an entirely different way from the minds of English speakers, it's not about their snowy experience. It's that whereas English speakers build up sentences using distinct (fairly short) words with (mostly) just a small amount of internal structure, speakers of a language like Kalaallisut often do a lot of the work of building a sentence by composing and inflecting a hugely complex verb that tells most of the story on its own.

## *On Whether Your Words Determine Your World*

The largely false tale of the many words for snow in Eskimoan languages often plays a role in discussions of what is commonly called the Sapir–Whorf Hypothesis. It's supposed to be a hypothesis about how language shapes or determines thought, but it isn't really a hypothesis at all. It's a vaguely defined cluster of very different claims.

Some variants appear to suggest that the way you think about the world is entirely determined by your language: a person who speaks a different language cannot think the same thoughts, and doesn't really even see the same world. Such an idea might seem fascinating at first. But on closer inspection it loses any claim to be a scientific thesis.

It has this curious property: if it were true, its truth could never be explained to the people it was true of. For example, if my language gave me a concept that you couldn't grasp because your language didn't equip you with that concept, I could never convince you that this was so, because you could never see what I meant. The key thing I would have to get across to you would involve a concept that you just don't have and cannot form.

That makes global claims of this sort (claims about our language defining our world) untestable even in principle. It's not a scientific hypothesis; it's a rather strange (and in my view implausible) metaphysical claim that no one can ever confirm or refute. That is part of why linguists are so much less intrigued by global Sapir–Whorf-style claims than nonlinguists.

There are testable claims about how language shapes thinking, however. They are much more modest, and generally involve tasks that involve speaking as well as thinking. For example, it has been shown that when someone has to sort a set of presented objects into their different colour categories, they can distinguish one shade of colour from another somewhat faster if their language has distinct words for those two shades.

But this only says that if you have lifelong experience with a language that uses a certain distinction as the crucial meaning difference between a pair of words, that may enhance the rapidity of your response to the distinction. It says nothing about your not being able to see the difference between a pair of colours that share the same word.

### Processing the Sentences You Hear

I stressed in Chapter 2 that language is not just words. Linguists are in general much more concerned with the issue of how utterances are processed, and how speakers' grasp of grammatical and semantic structure is implemented and acquired, than they are with the endless subtleties of word meaning.

In this area linguists work alongside psycholinguists. What has been discovered about the way we humans operate when we hear somebody say something is often truly surprising. For example, one might naïvely imagine that the way a sentence is processed is via a series of steps in this order:

- listen to the whole string of speech sounds;
- figure out which speech sounds were present (where you heard *s*, where it was *z*, etc.);
- identify the breaks between words (distinguishing *an arrow* from *a narrow*, for example);
- figure out the words intended at each point (e.g. whether a given word is *bear* or *bare*);
- look at the whole sequence of words and figure out how it fits together grammatically;
- compute the literal meaning of the sentence from the grammatical structure; and finally
- figure out how the literal meaning is relevant to you, and what you should infer about the speaker's intent.

What's interesting is not just that there are minor inaccuracies in this, but that essentially all of it is false. The instant you hear a speech sound, your mental record of all the words beginning with that sound becomes active in your brain. As the speech sounds keep coming, you eliminate possibilities at lightning speed. As each possible phrase is completed, you try associating it with all of its possible grammatical roles and literal meanings, simultaneously, and use facts about the present context to eliminate some of the alternatives. Before the speaker has even finished the sentence, you know virtually all you need to know about what's being said and what relevance it has. You basically have nothing left to do by the time you've heard the whole utterance.

If you think about it, this ties in with the fact that you've seen people finish other people's sentences, or begin their answer before they've heard all of the question. What's new is that psycholinguists have found various different ways to verify that this is happening, and to track it in real time. You can give people tasks designed to make them give unconscious clues to the way their mind is working. Under some conditions they may perform more quickly (or more slowly) at spotting whether some word or picture has come up on a screen; under some conditions their eye movements (tracked by an ingenious head-mounted device) may show that they looked back to a certain point while trying to read a sentence. It is even possible to read clues from traces of electrical activity picked up by sensors attached to points on their scalp that lie over particular regions of the brain.

Experimental psycholinguists, and linguists who work with them, have discovered types of sentence that cause the processing mechanisms to go temporarily haywire. Here's an example that will probably work on you, even though you have just been warned:

*The boy rushed out of the classroom shouted.*

Does that look ungrammatical? Did you assume I must have left out the word, probably *and*, just before *shouted*? Did you at least have a moment of doubt before realizing that there's nothing missing and nothing wrong with it at all?

The problem (if you experienced it) is that the sentence first tempts you to think we're talking about a boy who rushes out of a classroom. Then we bump into an apparent extra verb, *shouted*, and we don't know what to do with it. Adding *and* would make sense: he rushed out and shouted. However, this repair isn't necessary. The sentence is actually saying the boy was **being** rushed out (by teachers or paramedics or police who aren't mentioned), so he can be referred to as *the boy [who was] rushed out of the classroom*.

The reason this intelligibility problem can arise is that *the boy rushed out of the classroom* is inherently ambiguous: it can be a sentence or it can be a noun phrase. In the example I just discussed, the problem afflicts people who encounter a word (*rushed*) that could be the main verb of the sentence, and assume that it is.

## Words, Meaning, and Thought

Some sentences exhibit the opposite problem: a word that could be a noun is encountered early on, and you naturally assume it is a noun. It can happen even in very short sentences, like this one (again, this will probably bring you up short):

*The old man the ship often.*

Initially, it's baffling. You can imagine reading the words one by one, and going through explicit reasoning about how to understand the sentence, as shown in Table 2. We don't (normally) do any of this explicitly, of course, and I'm not suggesting that everyone knows terms like 'definite article', 'adjective', or 'relative clause'; but we are

Table 2

| WORDS HEARD SO FAR | WHAT YOU'RE SUBCONSCIOUSLY THINKING |
|---|---|
| *The* | (Definite article; beginning of a noun phrase.) |
| *The old* | (Adjective; probably modifying a noun that's coming up.) |
| *The old man* | (Confirmed: *old* is modifying *man*. Now I have a noun phrase.) |
| *The old man the* | (Noun followed by *the*? Maybe the start of a relative clause?) |
| *The old man the ship* | (Could still be right; looking for a verb now.) |
| *The old man the ship often.* | (That's it? Oops. I'm stumped now. No verb! Rethink?) |

61

apparently performing a subconscious analogue of this reasoning, at breakneck speed, every time we hear someone say something.

Naturally, frequency has something to do with our ability to understand sentences correctly. The word *man* is extremely common as a noun, and the adjective *old* often modifies it. To get the above sentence right you have to treat *the old* as a noun phrase meaning 'people who are old' and treat *man* as a verb meaning 'operate'.

Notice that it's much easier to understand *The old man the barricades*: the verb *man* is quite rare, but the *man the barricades* is common enough to give us a clue. We apparently have some subconscious sensitivity to the frequency with which one word is found adjacent to another.

What we're finding, then, is that the process of understanding things that people say to you is far from being a simple business of listening to a sequence of words and considering their meanings. What's going on is an extraordinarily complex process of trying to match the word sequence with at least three things: (i) constraints imposed by the grammar; (2) aspects of meaning and common sense that can help eliminate false trails; and (iii) subconsciously noticed probabilities of word sequences. You can probably see how crucial that could be for considerations ranging from language teaching to mental health evaluation to screenwriting to legal drafting to translation.

## *Applying Psycholinguistics*

The most important reasons why it is important that such aspects of human cognitive and linguistic abilities should be studied have to do with matters of education and health like learning deficits and brain injuries. Some people have real difficulties with processing language. Profound dyslexics have great difficulty distinguishing letter shapes and determining letter sequences. Patients with brain damage sometimes have partial or complete aphasia – inability to manage such things as the structure of sentences or the meanings of words. People with dementia or side effects of medication (as in the 'chemo brain' suffered by some chemotherapy patients) sometimes have impaired ability to comprehend and follow conversations. Some children have linguistic learning disabilities. And so on.

Without an expert understanding of the way human language processing mechanisms work, there is no hope of rationally based and rigorously defensible therapeutic work on helping such people.

Having a scientific understanding of linguistic systems and mechanisms is crucial for the medical profession to work out ways of helping people who have disabilities in the use of those systems and mechanisms.

An alien physiotherapist who didn't know that legs are used for locomotion, or that the lower leg should bend backward at the knee, or that the hip joint moves forward as well, and that the ankle should move in all directions, would be utterly incompetent. Physiotherapists need to know how legs work. Professionals in areas like aphasiology, neurology, and speech therapy need to know how the human language processing ability works.

Unfortunately, the integration of linguistic and psycholinguistic findings into such areas as education is the exception rather than the rule. Psycholinguist Mark Seidenberg, of the University of Wisconsin–Madison, has studied reading and literacy for many years, and has found the US educational establishment extraordinarily resistant to the discoveries that have been made through psycholinguistic experimentation. To cite just one example, although reading is secondary to speech, the two are extraordinarily closely tied together in the mind: a person's knowledge of sounds and letters are intimately enmeshed, and the answer to the

question of whether 'phonics' (the stressing of connections between letter strings and the sounds they
represent) should have a role in reading instruction is Yes. The US educational establishment has
largely decided that the answer should be No, and
they teach accordingly.

Seidenberg holds that commonly used methods
for teaching reading are inconsistent with what we
know about human cognition and development.
They make learning to read significantly more
difficult than it should be which has particularly
deleterious consequences for poorer children. Since
the body of research on reading happens to be deep
and broad and of high quality, he maintains, it is
particularly unfortunate that educators in the USA
pay so little attention to it.

# 4

# Language and Social Life

One evening in February 2012 an unarmed 17-year-old student walking home in Sanford, Florida, was shot dead 65 metres from his back door. The victim had been talking to a friend on the phone in real time, and reported being stalked.

Police, who were already on the way, arrived immediately and arrested the killer, who didn't deny what he'd done. The testimony of the victim's friend, a young woman named Rachel Jeantel, should have made the prosecution's case for a murder conviction virtually unassailable. But that's not how it went. Jeantel testified in her native dialect of English, and alienated not just the jury but thousands of TV viewers across the country.

We'll never know exactly what happened the night Trayvon Martin was shot. Jeantel testified that he was running away from his killer when he was shot. But the killer, George Zimmerman, a 28-year-old neighbourhood watch coordinator, claimed he was defending himself from a physical attack. And indeed, arrest photographs show him bleeding from the mouth and the back of the head. Still, you might expect at least a manslaughter conviction for a grown man who shoots an unarmed teenager dead over a fist fight. But instead the prosecution's star witness was reviled right across the country, and the jury returned a verdict of 'Not guilty' after deliberations in which Jeantel's evidence was never mentioned even once.

Rachel Jeantel speaks an interesting dialect that American linguists call African American Vernacular English (AAVE). There is powerful prejudice against it. Two Stanford University linguists, John Rickford and Sharese King, wrote an extended linguistic analysis of Jeantel's testimony and its reception. They argued that the crucial information she provided was disbelieved and ignored because of prejudice against the way she spoke. Jurors claimed she was 'hard to understand' and 'not credible'. She was on the stand for six hours, but her speech as heard on TV and radio led to her being not just dismissed but vilified as an idiot by social media users across the United States.

Typical white middle-class speakers of standard English, and even educated African Americans, regard AAVE as simply sloppy, careless, bad English. A fairly mild contributor to the storm of hostile commentary aimed at Jeantel after her testimony wrote on Twitter:

> Everyone, regardless of race, should learn to speak correct English, or at least UNDERSTANDABLE English . . . I couldn't understand 75% of what she was saying . . . that is just ridicolous! [*sic*]

If the commenter had studied standard French in school and subsequently found that she couldn't follow native speakers chatting in colloquial Parisian, she would presumably blame her own lack of experience. But when someone fails to follow a native speaker of AAVE, the allegation of language-learning failure goes in the other direction.

AAVE has an awkward sociological and legal status. Though not always mutually intelligible with the most broadly accepted varieties of English in the USA, it is not recognized as a distinct language either. Its own speakers always describe themselves as speaking English. Defence lawyer Don West asked Jeantel about her command of English, and her indignant answer was 'I understand English really well.'

Jeantel is in fact trilingual: she knows Haitian Kweyol and Dominican Spanish, having a Haitian mother and a Dominican father. But she was a 19-year-old high school student in 2012, not a sophisticated adult with skills in switching between English dialects. And unfortunately the jurors were not acquainted with AAVE. Nor were the lawyers, or the judge. Yet given that AAVE speakers (including Jeantel herself) insist that AAVE is simply English, the possibility of having a court interpreter never even arose.

## *Nonstandard Dialects and Despised Languages*

Notice that when I use the term 'nonstandard' here, it's not a value judgement. Linguists describe the extent to which the dialects under discussion here differ from standard English in some grammatical and phonological properties, but that doesn't at all imply that they are **sub**standard dialects. Nor does it imply that using standard English is always better. That depends on the conversation you want to have, the task that confronts you, the impression you want to create.

Using a nonstandard dialect is often preferable (for those who know how) to using standard

English. Think of a salesman trying to get on good terms with a vernacular-using customer or a doctor trying put a nonstandard dialect speaker at her ease; writing the lyrics for a country song; rousing audience support at a political rally; relaxing with country relatives; telling a comic anecdote; talking on the first day of school to a scared five-year-old child who has hardly ever heard standard English before ... Not every expert English user wants to sound like Prince Charles all the time.

And the fact that dialects and languages have their own integrity and structure and dignity can make a huge difference to the way people feel about themselves. My friend Habib, a highly educated Tunisian computer scientist, told me he had been profoundly changed by a linguistics course that he once took. After some aspects of grammar had been examined in detail in the class, he suddenly saw that he had always thought of himself as someone who spoke shamefully bad Arabic. He knew what modern standard Arabic sounded like, and read it in the newspapers, and (in an older version) in the holy Qur'an, and he knew that what he spoke every day with his family was strikingly different. But suddenly he realized that he and his family weren't speaking bad Arabic at all; they were speaking fluent, perfect Tunisian.

Habib was right. The Tunisian member of the Arabic language family is not the same as colloquial Cairo Egyptian Arabic, or colloquial Iraqi, or Lebanese, or the modern literary language that serves as the medium for learned discourse all over the Arabic world. That doesn't mean that Tunisian is bad, or that Tunisians are ill-schooled hicks. Tunisian is a language too, and Habib spoke it perfectly. He was just fine the way he was. Especially given that he knows standard Arabic and English as well. He's an educated trilingual raised in Tunisia, but had grown up thinking of himself as an ignorant mangler of Arabic.

## The Field of Sociolinguistics

The connection between languages and the societies within which they are used is so intimate and so intricate that since the early 1960s a whole field within the language sciences has grown up devoted to exploring it. It's called sociolinguistics. And it has yielded perhaps the most important results and significant applications of any part of linguistics.

One of its originators was William Labov at the University of Pennsylvania. He made his name with a book on the way dialects in New York City correlated with class. He found by personal experimentation that getting a shop floor assistant in a department store to say a couple of words such as 'fourth floor' was enough for you to tell what the price levels would be: in the fancier stores the staff are more likely to pronounce *r* after a vowel in the characteristic American way, but in lower-class stores they tend to have accents without the *r*.

Labov was an early pioneer in the linguistic study of AAVE. Many others have followed him in studying its grammar and phonology, and today there is a considerable fund of knowledge about it. AAVE is one of the languages in which sentences with meanings like *He is angry* or *You are a fool* do not always have a word corresponding to the verb *be* – the verb that in standard English has forms including *be*, *am*, *is*, *are*, *was*, *were*, and so on. It is often referred to as the copula, and I'll use that term here. Crucially, the copula is not just omitted in sentences like *He angry* or *You a fool* through laziness, or ignorance of what's 'correct'. There is a grammatical rule in operation. An approximate statement would be this:

Optionally omit the copula provided it is
(a) tensed (so forms like *be* and *been* are not
    dropped),

(b) in a present tense form (so *was* and *were* are not dropped),

(c) in the second or third person (so *am* is not dropped),

(d) not sufffixed by *-n't* (so forms like *ain't* are not dropped),

(e) not emphatically stressed (so *is* would not be dropped in *There already is one*), and

(f) not the last word in its clause or phrase (so the *is* would not be dropped in *what it is*).

This complex grammatical generalization about where the copula is to be omitted is part of the unconscious command of the dialect that its native speakers have. Anyone who wanted to speak AAVE would have to learn the rules – just as they would have to learn the relevant rules if they wanted to speak Russian or Hungarian, both of which are languages that in certain contexts do not use a verb corresponding to English *be*.

There are other clear differences between AAVE and standard English. In AAVE the auxiliary often precedes the subject in a negative declarative clause, and a clause cannot be negated simply by a noun phrase like *nobody*, but must have a negative auxiliary verb in addition; so standard English *Nobody has time for that* translates as *Ain't nobody got time for that*.

Consider translating into AAVE the standard English sentence *There are no batteries in it*. This is an existential clause. You need to know that in AAVE the first word should be *it* rather than *there*. And inflectional endings like the *-s* of plural nouns (*dogs*) and the *-'s* of genitive nouns (*dog's* or *dogs'*) are typically absent (almost 100% of the time in Rachel Jeantel's AAVE). Respecting these rules and the others relevant to negated clauses, the AAVE translation would be *It ain't no battery in it*.

And so on. The point is that AAVE has detailed grammatical rules, many similar to those of standard English but some clearly different. AAVE is not (as too many people believe) just messed-up English.

The connection of such grammatical facts to sociolinguistics (and the reason I'm discussing them here rather than in Chapter 2) is that people's attitudes toward AAVE make doing the work of identifying the rules quite tricky socially. Nearly all speakers of the language are black Americans who can often speak varieties of English much closer to standard English, and vary their speech according to the social context. Sometimes they are rather ashamed of coming from a family that uses AAVE. Usually they won't speak it in front of some stranger doing sociolinguistic research. You can ask a bilingual in, say, English and Greek, 'How would you say that in Greek?' Similar direct questions about a nonstandard dialect do not yield reliable results.

The Cambridge linguist W. Sidney Allen once stated that 'the linguist's gospel comprises every word that proceeds from his informant's mouth – which cannot, by definition, be wrong', whereas 'as a matter of principle, whatever the informant volunteers *about* his language (as opposed to in it) must be assumed to be wrong.' This overstates things somewhat (speakers can commit slips of the tongue, and they're not 100% wrong in what they say about their language), but the warning is a valid one: the way people actually speak is the object of study, and we cannot assume that people are correct when they make a claim about their own language use. People often deny using nonstandard forms or casual speech forms. They may imagine that they never say *Get 'em* for *Get them*, and so on. When a linguist shows them evidence that they are mistaken – sometimes even evidence from recordings of their own speech – they are shocked or even emotionally upset.

There is even more room for people to be mistaken or defensive about their own patterns of speech when they constantly hear standard English but regularly use AAVE, and to some extent interleave or mix the two dialects or switch between them, and have never thought of AAVE as something to be described with care, but have often been told that it is 'bad English' and they should be ashamed of speaking it. It's just like Habib with Tunisian. Helping to heal the damage done to people by others' contempt for their native language is one of the fortunate side effects emerging from work in sociolinguistics.

## *The Asymmetry of Intelligibility*

Sociolinguists, equipped with the kind of skills possessed by anthropologists and social psychologists, often conduct research on topics like the properties of nonstandard dialects or low-prestige languages; they are a natural laboratory for all sorts of phenomena that sociolinguists want to study. And some of the things they have discovered about nonstandard dialects and low-prestige languages strike me as extremely important in practical terms.

It would be very natural to expect the relation of intelligibility between languages or dialects to be symmetric. That is, it would be very reasonable to think that if speakers of language *A* can understand speakers of language *B*, then naturally speakers of language *B* will be able to understand speakers of language *A*. It seems obvious. But it's not true. In a 1959 paper the linguist Hans Wolff reported this about Nembe and Kalabari, two West African languages so similar that a linguist would classify them as dialects of a single language:

> The intelligibility data curiously contradicts expectations based on comparability. The Nembe freely acknowledge the similarity of the Kalabari dialects to their own and claim to be able to understand speakers of Kalabari. The latter, however, claim that Nembe is a very different language, unintelligible except for scattered word recognition. They answer Nembe claims of intelligibility by maintaining that this would be possible only if any given speaker of Nembe had taken the trouble to learn Kalabari. At the same time they haughtily dismiss as extremely unlikely and farfetched the idea that any Kalabari should bother to learn Nembe. All efforts of the writer to reach some kind of compromise in this area were fruitless, and separate orthographies had to be set up for the two groups.

Why would that be? Wolff goes on to observe that nonlinguistic factors are involved:

> The Kalabari are by far the largest and economically most prosperous group in the eastern Delta. They regard the Nembe [. . .] as poor country cousins, definitely inferior to themselves.

So the prosperous Kalabari pay little heed to the poorer Nembe people and either have not learned to understand them, or do not care to learn. The Nembe, by contrast, pay attention to what the more prosperous Kalabari people say, and report being able to understand them. Now the linguistic science begins to reconcile with the social science. The two languages are so closely related, and so grammatically and phonologically similar, that if you know one of them you could easily understand the other if you just paid close attention to it. But although the indigent pay close attention to what the wealthy say (there could always be some advantage to gain), the rich don't have to pay any attention to the way the poor talk; why bother about them. That's how you can have two languages, demonstrably almost identical in linguistic terms, with the intelligibility between them going in one direction only.

## All Languages Great and Small

I've given a couple of examples where I think society really does have a stake (more than almost anybody realizes) in fine-detail analysis of what a language is actually like, or what a piece of language says. But to a large extent the importance of linguistics has turned out to lie not so much in the results it has achieved (those evolve over time and are often overturned or contradicted) but in the change in the general view of what's important enough to study. It lies in the moral evolution of our perception of what we should be looking at and what we should value. One interesting example concerns sign languages.

Not too many decades ago people thought the sign communication used by the deaf was just a sort of inchoate gesticulation to get vague wants and feelings across. Teachers disapproved of signing; they even punished children for doing it. Lip-reading and written communication were stressed to the complete exclusion of anything involving gesture. It was not until linguists started getting seriously into the analysis of sign communication systems that it became fully clear just how much these full-scale human languages have in common with the spoken ones. Pioneers like Edward Klima and Ursula Bellugi were not just acquainting themselves with a field of linguistic study but creating a new one when they started working on American Sign Language.

It is only the externalization medium that defines a radical break between the two kinds of language: oral production and aural perception for speech, gestural production and visual perception for sign.

Linguists today actually speak of 'sign-language phonology', not because they don't understand that the *phono-* bit derives from the Greek root meaning 'voice' but because they have discovered that the micro-detail of sign production closely parallels phonology. True sign languages use actions with the fingers, hands, wrists, arms, shoulders, and face in highly complex and minutely articulated movements that take the place of the phonetics and phonology of spoken languages. Interestingly, fluent users of sign language do not look at the hands of their interlocutor: they look at the face, letting their peripheral vision pick up the information from the hand and arm movements. Embedded in the flow of gestures are subtle influences of each sign on the form of the next. There are structural constraints on the overall shape of a sign, and syntactic structures within which the signs fit just as pronounced words relate to grammar in a spoken language.

The signs are not some kind of spelled-out substitute for speech. (Occasionally a word in some written language has to be spelled out because there is no established sign translation, but that is not the normal case.) Nor are most signs iconic representations of the way things look. Some signs have an iconic aspect (a hand movement toward the mouth to suggest eating, perhaps, or a movement toward the ground to suggest a concept like 'down' or 'below'); but some signs are apparently arbitrary, with hand shapes and arm movements telling you nothing about what a sign stands for semantically, just as the sound of a word normally tells you nothing about its meaning (*big* is a very little word, while *microscopic* is quite a large one; onomatopoeia as in *bang* or *whoosh* is rare). But the crucial point is that sign languages have their own grammar: subjects, objects, verbs, adverbs, conditions on how they are put together, and so on.

Reports of success in teaching sign languages to non-human primates have been absurdly exaggerated. Videos have been made of efforts to teach American Sign Language to chimpanzees like Washoe and Nim Chimpsky, and to a gorilla named Koko. No one could mistake them for evidence of fluent human sign-language use. Although apes have been painstakingly taught to use at least some hand signs, they seem to use them mainly when mimicking signs made by their trainers moments before, and they never combine them into sentences expressing statements or questions. Compare even half a minute of a human sign-language interpreter on TV with any of the fragmentary footage of occasional sign production by apes, and you will see that the question of whether the apes are doing anything similar to signing in American Sign Language is not even worth discussing. I regard it as grossly insulting to the native speakers of sign languages to suggest otherwise. You will not find professional linguists talking about Washoe or Nim or Koko uttering sign-language sentences.

Sign languages, creole languages, and vernacular dialects all instantiate the same human capacity for linguistic expression. Understanding in full detail how they are used in subtle ways, not just to talk about arbitrary subject matters but also to signal identity and social status, is not just a pursuit to be pursued for its own sake by academics; it opens up new vistas of understanding concerning social structure and human diversity.

# 5

# Machines That Understand Us

'Open the pod bay doors, HAL.'
*'I'm sorry, Dave. I'm afraid I can't do that.'*
'What's the problem?'
*'I think you know what the problem is just as well as I do.'*

Everyone who has seen *2001: A Space Odyssey* remembers that chilling scene. Dave Bowman is locked out in deep space by the misguided zeal of an artificially intelligent machine that the crew addresses as HAL. It has defined him as a threat to the mission who must be eliminated.

In fluent and graceful English, HAL apologizes for declining an order, addressing Dave by name, and talks about the refusal to open the doors politely, referring idiomatically to a mental state of regret ('I'm afraid. . .'). HAL even displays an understanding of Dave's likely state of mind ('I think you know. . .'). What makes it all so scary is that HAL forms complete thoughts based on comprehension of the current situation, and expresses them with precision, even intuiting a human's mind state.

When the film was released in 1968, the eponymous year 2001 seemed unimaginably far off. But 17-year-old filmgoers had only to wait a year to see actual men landing on the moon (that came in July 1969), and were still only 50 when the real 2001 arrived. Since then another generation has been born, grown up, and left school. Yet not only are there no regular flights to the moon (nobody has been back there since 1972), let alone bases there, but in all of our technology we see nothing like HAL's linguistic ability in robots, computers, smartphones, or other appliances. You cannot even ask a computer a simple question in error-free English by email and get an answer by return.

Back in the 1980s it looked as if machine recognition of connected speech would be the biggest stumbling block: separating out the words from a continuous stream of highly variable acoustic mush seemed a truly intractable task. Sensible handling of typed-in sentences looked much easier, because plenty was known about English grammar and parsing algorithms. Instead, it was speech recognition that was conquered. Remarkable successes were achieved with the aid of huge libraries of statistical facts about speech, clever algorithms for statistical computation, and hardware with gigabytes of RAM and disk space. Machines are now very good at guessing which words you just said, even over the phone, especially if trained up on a sample of your speech. Meanwhile we are virtually nowhere with understanding of written sentences. The devices that can guess which words you uttered have relatively little they can do with those words: they exhibit not a flicker of actual linguistic understanding.

Plenty of ingenuity goes into attempts at concealing this fact. A minor but entertaining aspect of the business is the embedding of large numbers of tricks and surprises, called 'Easter eggs', into interactive voice-driven software. If you address Apple's 'Siri', or Amazon's 'Alexa', or Microsoft's 'Cortana', and ask them to open the pod bay doors, you will generally get some sort of response based on *2001*. At one point Google's 'Allo' messenger app was programmed to tell you that there is a spare key under the flower pot outside the pod bay airlock so you can let yourself in. And Siri, the voice-responsive agent on the iPhone, famously has lots of witty built-in responses for people who profess love or propose marriage or ask for a sandwich or seek enlightenment on whether there is a god.

These tricks depend entirely on massive data storage: a library of tens of thousands of stored answers to questions that people often ask. You can think of it as a vast list of pairs, the first member of each pair being an utterance (actually, just a numerically represented description of a class of similar noise bursts) and the second member being an instruction regarding what should be fed to the audio output if the first member is recognized. Some of them are Easter eggs, as shown in Table 3. Others are sensible answers to much more boring questions, or triggers for making the device run suitable searches: *Where can we eat around here?* might trigger a map search for businesses listed as restaurants within a mile of the phone's current location, and so on. But this kind of automatic triggering of mechanical responses has nothing to do with understanding of sentences. It's just faking, based primarily on a statistical understanding of questions people

**Table 3**

| IF THIS IS RECOGNIZED: | OUTPUT THIS: |
| --- | --- |
| *Do you believe in God?* | *I eschew theological disquisition.* |
| *Will you marry me?* | *Let's just be friends, OK?* |
| *Make me a sandwich.* | *I can't. I have no condiments.* |
| *Set phasers to kill.* | *That's a feature for a later version.* |
| . . . | . . . |

commonly ask. Mark Steedman, a computational linguist, has described statistics-based information retrieval as 'getting better and better at recalling what is already well-known, and understanding what has often been said before.'

## *The Words in the Box*

Over the last ten years, Google has been steadily modifying its search engine to provide sensible answers to huge numbers of commonly asked questions (thereby in effect underscoring Steedman's point). Consider what happens if you put this in the Google search box (I omit all punctuation and capitalization from examples of search box words to remind you that Google strips away all such information before starting work anyway):

> what is the square root of 6389

If you had typed that in at an earlier stage of Google's history, it would just have called up a list of URLs for pages containing the character-strings *6389*, *root*, *square*, and *what*. (It makes virtually no difference to include the words *is*, *of*, and *the*, because they occur in essentially every page, of course: words as ubiquitous as that could simply be ignored.) It would then have ordered the pages with the most influential ones at the top of the list. But today it presents highly relevant pages about finding square roots, and at the top an actual answer to the question, presented on the display of a usable on-screen calculator.

However, **it doesn't do this on the basis of understanding what the question said.**

It can't involve recognizing full sentences from a list, because it seems to work with any arbitrary number. The trick it is using involves matching common frames: for any word sequence matching the pattern *what is the . . . of . . .*, Google is rigged to fetch the calculator if the first blank is the name of some common one-place mathematical function like 'square root' and the second is a sequence of digits.

The programming seems to have been set up to deal with hundreds (perhaps thousands) of such patterns. If the first blank is filled with *capital* or *capital city*, Google will instantly (even before you finish typing your question) assume that the second blank should be looked up on a list of countries, states, provinces, and counties. Type 'U' and it starts making suggestions for filling that second slot (USA? Ukraine? Uruguay? Uganda? UK?).

Then on recognizing any country or state name (or even a common misspelling of such a name) it will instantly present a box of information about the relevant capital city.

However, presenting the words of a question in some random order produces roughly the same front page of results, including the information box. But randomly ordering the words tends to get more hits (maybe ten times as many) rather than fewer. That is because Google's algorithm pays attention not just to individual words but to subsequences of the list of words in the box. Frequent subsequences like *what is* and *capital of* narrow the search considerably. When the order of the words in the box provides very few clues, statistical facts about word co-occurrence have to suffice. The probability of someone putting Uzbekistan and capital and what in the same box and not wanting information about Tashkent is extraordinarily low (and anyway, no harm is done by including a box of information about Tashkent on the front page of results, even if there is a faint possibility that the user might not need it).

None of this involves anything like understanding English sentences. There is no appeal to English grammatical structure (that *what* is a pronoun used in interrogative clauses, that *is* belongs to the class of auxiliary verbs, that the auxiliary comes before the subject noun phrase under certain conditions in interrogative clauses, etc.). Human speakers of English subconsciously rely on general principles which can help permit the comprehension of questions even about totally improbable or unexpected things. Google cannot do that at all; it is limited to common question frames that hundreds of thousands of users have presented in previous searches.

## *Chatbots with Secret Languages?*

I've been stressing the absence of genuine language processing in current web-search technology because most people are far too ready to believe that computers understand them. They seem to imagine that at least some aspects of the meaning of the questions they type into the Google box are actually understood. They may even believe that Google's computers read and understand the emails they send via Gmail. They are, in short, astonishingly willing to believe that computers are engaged in thinking and understanding. But they aren't.

In 2017, Facebook did some research, widely reported in the press, to see if two chatbots (computer programs intended to simulate conversation) could learn how to negotiate pricing of some imaginary commodities – balls, hats, and books. On one run, as the pseudo-conversation proceeded, it started looking like this:

**Bob**: i can i i everything else . . .
**Alice**: balls have zero to me to me to me to me to me to me to me to me to
**Bob**: you i everything else . . .
**Alice**: balls have a ball to me to me to me to me to me to me to me

And journalists wrote stories about how the experiment had to be terminated because the bots were evolving a new language that the scientists couldn't understand. *Newsweek* went so far as to say that it was beginning to look as if a negotiation bot could turn into 'a potential monster: a bot that can cut deals with no empathy for people, says whatever it takes to get what it wants, hacks language so no one is sure what it's communicating and can't be distinguished from a human being.' It went on: 'If we're not careful, a bot like that could rule the world.'

Are journalists gullible enough to truly believe this stuff? Or do they write such nonsense because they know we'll lap it up like kittens at a saucer of milk? The lesson from the two bots' flailing, illustrated above, is that when extremely complex computer programs are trained to become familiar with the patterns found in huge bodies of complex data, and are programmed to feed results about their own performance back into their own further learning, they will produce strange and apparently random effects whenever they are put in a situation where no sensible output is determined by their training regimes. The babblings they produce mean absolutely nothing.

Related phenomena had been observed some months before when people noticed that giving Google Translate meaningless repetitive sequences to translate could lead to weird and apparently random outputs, rather like strange modern poetry. One investigator found that asking for *nu nu* to be translated from Japanese into English yielded the output *unlikely*; but *nu nu nu* produced *muco* (that means 'mucus' in Spanish and Italian); *nu nu nu nu* yielded *a lukewarm*; *nu nu nu nu nu* translated as *a rainy season*; and so it went on, with progressively more and more outlandish results.

Typing *nu* twenty-eight times produced the output *evening a cute buttery crown*. That does not mean there is any connection between the meaningless sequence and the meaning of 'evening a cute buttery crown', still less that Google Translate thought there was. The output was just a quasi-random consequence of driving an extraordinarily complex computer program into realms where its training gave it no precedent to rely on and did not permit it to do anything sensible or useful.

## *What Machine Question-Answering Would Be Like*

Google Translate is of course not even trying to do anything that remotely resembles understanding sentences. Nor does the Google search engine even pretend to try to understand the sequence of words you put in the box. One way to show this is to take a question with a trivially obvious answer that doesn't need anything to be looked up. Try putting this in the Google search box:

| do people who need people need people |
| --- |

There are tens of thousands of hits, all the most highly ranked ones being pages about Barbra Streisand and/or the 1964 song 'People' by Jule Styne and Bob Merrill. There is no sign of the answer, which is of course 'Yes'.

Another way to bring out the fact that questions are not being understood is with a sentence like this one:

> which states in america have no land
> neighbours

It brings up a slew of pages – hundreds of thousands of them – about all sorts of topics relating to things like borders, countries, states, neighbours, land neighbours, New Zealand, China, America, Zambia, boundary disputes, landlocked countries . . . but no sign of the correct answer: Hawaii and Alaska. It is as if Google is flailing around desperately trying to find something that might help us, and failing utterly. Because what's going on, of course, is that phrases are not being understood: *states in America* is not recognized as a phrase limiting attention to just the states of the USA, and above all, *no land neighbours* is not being recognized as a phrase denoting the opposite of *some land neighbours* (in the sense that *have no land neighbours* applies to exactly those states to which *have some land neighbours* doesn't apply, and vice versa).

But it's not only indications of negation like *no* or *not* that cause this kind of trouble with finding answers via Google. Consider this example:

> which states border american states which
> border texas

It elicits the URLs of hundreds of thousands of pages about states, borders, Texas, migrants, Mexico, etc. – but not a hint of the answer.

Yet it would be relatively easy for a computer to take such strings of words, treat them as questions, and work out the answers. Let's look very briefly at how it might be done in a couple of cases.

We'll start with *Do people who need people need people?* – a type of clause that grammarians call a closed interrogative because the set of legitimate answers is a closed list that depends on the form of the sentence. In this case the list contains just 'Yes' and 'No'. Let's think through the way in which a computer could figure out that the correct answer is 'Yes'.

*People* denotes the collection of all human beings; *need people* is a verb phrase expressing the property of finding contact with human beings necessary. Call that property $p_1$. The words *who need people* make up a relative clause that can alter the reference of a noun that it modifies, cutting it down to a subset with the property $p_1$. So *people who need people* picks out the set of humans who have $p_1$.

Call that set $H$. The question asks for a decision on whether the members of $H$ have $p_1$. And of course they all do, by the definition of $H$. So the answer is 'Yes'.

Now let's consider an open interrogative. A linguistically appropriate answer to an open interrogative is chosen from an indefinitely large list. If we consider *Which states border American states which border Texas?* as our sentence, an appropriate answer will be a list of state names. To find the states on the list corresponding to the correct answer we first need to understand the verb *border*. One state borders another if and only if a line can be drawn from a point in one of them to a point in the other that crosses only one state boundary. A glance at a map shows that lines crossing into Texas (TX) can be drawn from New Mexico (NM), Oklahoma (OK), Arkansas (AS), or Louisiana (LA). A database recording such information could be as simple as a list of pairs of adjacent states: $\langle$NM, TX$\rangle$, $\langle$OK, TX$\rangle$, $\langle$AS, TX$\rangle$, $\langle$LA, TX$\rangle$, and so on. (Note that whenever $\langle X, Y \rangle$ is in the database, $\langle Y, X \rangle$ must also be in it, because you can drive between two adjacent states in either direction.) One computer programmer, under the pseudonym 'ubikuity', wrote a computer program to construct such a database from published sources, and published it on GitHub.[*]

Answering our question means supplying a list containing every state $S$ such that $\langle S, \text{TX} \rangle$ (and therefore also $\langle \text{TX}, S \rangle$) is in the database. Let's consider how you could get to that from the sentence under consideration.

Linguists make diagrams of sentence structure known as trees. A tree is a set of labelled points connected by lines called branches. There is a unique point called the root (conventionally drawn at the top) from which you can reach any of the other points by travelling down sequences of branches. Each point is labelled with the name of a category of word or phrase. The structure of *Which states border American states which border Texas?* could be represented by Figure 1. Each sequence of words that forms a coherent part of the sentence gets a unique label above it indicating its grammatical category: *American states* is a Noun Phrase, *border Texas* is a Verb Phrase, *Texas* is another Noun Phrase (with only one component, a Noun), and so on. These category-labelled sequences are called constituents. (Notice that a sequence like *states*

---

[*] See: https://github.com/ubikuity/List-of-neighboring-states-for-each-US-state.

*which* isn't a constituent and thus doesn't get a label of its own: it's just an accidental juxtaposition of the second half of a Noun Phrase constituent and the first word of a Relative Clause constituent.)

A diagram of this sort can be constructed rapidly and efficiently from a sequence of words by a computer program given access to a grammar with rules like 'a Verb Phrase may consist of a Verb and a Noun Phrase', 'a Noun Phrase may consist of a Noun Phrase and a Relative Clause', and so on.

There is enough information in Figure 1 for a computer program to work out what to do to answer the question, given only a database of states and their neighbours. It will seem a bit brain-bending to look at when I lay it out, but it represents just the kind of problem that computers are brilliant at – and you are too, because you do such computations every second when people are talking to you. Table 4 shows the most significant constituents, with identification letters (**A** to **F**) for ease of reference, and grammatical category labels, and indications of its meaning (or to be specific, of denotation – other layers of meaning are ignored here).

A computer program could build up a representation of the full meaning of the clause (at **F** in Table 4) starting from the individual parts in Figure 1. Given access to the database, it could answer the

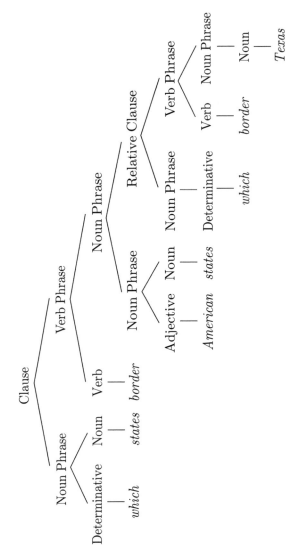

**Figure 1**

99

**Table 4**

| ID | WORD SEQUENCE | CATEGORY | REFERS TO |
|----|---------------|----------|-----------|
| A | *American states* | Noun Phrase | collection of all fifty states of the USA |
| B | *border Texas* | Verb Phrase | property of being a state from which you can drive directly into Texas over one boundary |
| C | *which border Texas* | Relative Clause | condition requiring the property **B** |
| D | *American states which border Texas* | Noun Phrase | members of **A** that meet condition **C** |
| E | *border American states which border Texas* | Verb Phrase | property of being a state from which you can pass directly into one of the states denoted by **D** |
| F | *which states border American states which border Texas* | Clause | question asking for the states that have the property **E** |

question. To determine whether Arizona has the property **E** (it borders a state which borders Texas) you simply need to find a state *S* such that ⟨AZ, *S*⟩ is in the database and so is ⟨*S*, TX⟩. And *S* = NM gives you that. Therefore Arizona has the property **E**, and is on the list that the question asks for.

Working out the meaning of a sentence like the one we have just considered, and looking up the answer to the question, would be trivially easy for a computer program. Provided it could do the syntactic analysis that leads to the structure shown in Figure 1.

## *The Demand for Natural Language Processing*

I've just given a very brief look at how a computer might actually answer a question. The question this raises is whether at some point the general public will start expecting programs that can do such things. Google seems to satisfy most users at present. It probably achieves something like 90% success in its mission, which gets people fairly close to the point of being able to find for themselves an answer to whatever question they have in mind, and will serve most people's needs, most of the time, for a few years. But there is real doubt about how much of the remaining 10% or so it will be able to handle using the same methods.

Eventually, I believe, people will find they feel a need to make inroads into that missing 10%. The public's hunger for access to information is insatiable, and people increasingly want it fast: they are disinclined to spend time scouring web pages full of irrelevant stuff. Modern computers have all the power and speed that would be needed to actually answer questions, rather than simply put people in the presence of a list of web pages in which the answer might or might not be found. And almost everyone is used to typing sentences on a keyboard (or a keyboard substitute, as on a phone). We will eventually want our computers to understand questions asked in plain English sentences.

When that time comes, the information industry will need to draw on the work that linguists have been doing during the past half-century. It will be critical to have fully precise definitions of the syntactic rules of English, and principles for computing the literal meaning of any sentence that the rules permit. At that point, the information industry will need linguistics. And for linguists, it will be the point where the rubber hits the road: we will find out whether current understanding of sentence structure and meaning is adequate to the task of being incorporated into working systems. In other words, whether the science of linguistics is well enough developed to support engineering.

Once questions can be fully and accurately understood, other uses of computerized grammatical analysis will emerge, such as proofreading and checking for unintentional typing slips. You might think we already have it, because there are some commercial products (including Microsoft Word) that claim to provide it. But their performance is largely hopeless.

I did a small experiment to check on my anecdotal recollections of past experience. Selecting a book at random, I put its first few sentences into a Microsoft Word file, mutilated them by removing all even-numbered seven-word sequences, and then checked it with the grammar checker built into Word for Mac version 15.17 (151206). The text I chose was the first three sentences of Oscar Wilde's luxuriantly literary novella *The Picture of Dorian Gray*:

> The studio was filled with the rich odour of roses, and when the light summer wind stirred amidst the trees of the garden, there came through the open door the heavy scent of the lilac, or the more delicate perfume of the pink-flowering thorn. From the corner of the divan of Persian saddle-bags on which

he was lying, smoking, as was his custom, innumerable cigarettes, Lord Henry Wotton could just catch the gleam of the honey-sweet and honey-coloured blossoms of a laburnum, whose tremulous branches seemed hardly able to bear the burden of a beauty so flamelike as theirs; and now and then the fantastic shadows of birds in flight flitted across the long tussore-silk curtains that were stretched in front of the huge window, producing a kind of momentary Japanese effect, and making him think of those pallid, jade-faced painters of Tokyo who, through the medium of an art that is necessarily immobile, seek to convey the sense of swiftness and motion. The sullen murmur of the bees shouldering their way through the long unmown grass, or circling with monotonous insistence round the dusty gilt horns of the straggling woodbine, seemed to make the stillness more oppressive.

Word reported no errors except to query the spelling of two words not in its dictionary, *flamelike* and *tussore*. I then garbled it by omitting every even-numbered seven-word sequence (leaving out words 8–14, 22–8, 36–42, etc.), to produce the following shorter passage of absolute gibberish:

The studio was filled with the rich summer wind stirred amidst the trees of door the heavy scent of the lilac, pink-flowering thorn. From the corner

104

of the was lying, smoking, as was his custom, catch the gleam of the honey-sweet and branches seemed hardly able to bear the theirs; and now and then the fantastic the long tussore-silk curtains that were stretched a kind of momentary Japanese effect, and painters of Tokyo who, through the medium seek to convey the sense of swiftness bees shouldering their way through the long round the dusty gilt horns of the more oppressive.

Astonishingly, Word reported no errors at all in this. Word's grammar-checking is extremely primitive, largely limited to spotting phrase types that are stereotypically deprecated, or very simple agreement errors. It does get a few things right: I found on my machine that if given George W. Bush's famous slip *Is our children learning?* (recall that I use an asterisk prefix to signal an ungrammatical sentence) it would correctly suggest changing *is* to *are*; but then again, given *I do not work as a teachers* it suggested correcting it to *I do not work as some teachers*. It passed whole paragraphs of deliberately constructed nonsense without anything flagging any of the deliberate errors. Personally I find it an almost completely useless tool. There could hardly be a more direct illustration of the need for applying what linguists have found out about sentence structure in the last few decades.

Not even spelling can be checked reliably (though we desperately need help there, given the gross inconsistencies and complications of the English spelling system). Current products are almost entirely limited to spotting individual letter strings that are not in the dictionary. There are few signs yet of spell-checking that can spot (for example) where you meant *bare* but typed *bear*. Sometimes using one instead of the other makes a sentence ungrammatical: *The landscape looked completely bare* is grammatical, but *\*The landscape looked completely bear* is not. And *Outside the cabin we saw a brown bear* is grammatical, but *\*Outside the cabin we saw a brown bare* is not. I'm not aware of any commercially available spell-checker that will systematically catch errors of that kind.

Even if we limit ourselves to extremely elementary help with the technical side of writing, current word processing and editing software offers us hardly any grammar-based assistance. Consider the common mistake of opening a parenthesis for some interruption of a sentence and then ending the sentence inside the parenthesis instead of outside it. To find a real-life example to show you, I dipped into a collection of two million *Wall Street Journal* sentences often used for testing by computational linguists. The twelfth occurrence of a full stop followed by a right parenthesis was this one, which illustrates the mistake:

> *Critics claim, however, that St. Petersburg lacks enough hotel rooms to support the conventions (though Mr. Obering believes the stadium will encourage construction of more.)*

I only needed to read twelve of the roughly 15,000 sentences containing '.)' – that's 0.08% of them – in order to find an erroneous case. That suggests the error might be quite common. It could easily be corrected by a program sensitive to sentence boundaries and parentheses. But even getting that far calls for some serious linguistics. The definition of 'sentence' isn't just something like 'capital letter followed by sequence of letters and numbers and non-final punctuation marks and ended by a sentence-ending punctuation mark'. Some full stops mark abbreviations (*etc.*; *Con.*; *Mr.*; *i.e.*; *U.K.*; and thousands of other cases). Simple-minded definitions will give the wrong results. Figuring out where sentences begin and end involves serious grammatical analysis of the kind familiar to researchers in linguistics.

Only with a great deal of collaboration between linguists and software engineers can we ever reach the stage of having word processor technology (or other text-sensitive software: typesetting machinery, blogging platforms, text-to-speech systems, optical character recognition programs, etc.) that can do text-checking on a non-trivial level. Machine proofreading even for simple mechanical aspects of grammar and punctuation is simply beyond today's technology. If we want it, precise modelling of fine detail will be crucial, and linguistics is going to have a major role to play.

## *Conversing with Robots*

Far beyond the realm of elementary language understanding tasks lies actual conversation with computer programs and ultimately robots. Here we confront the curious fact that it is far easier to fool users into thinking it has been accomplished in full than it is to actually achieve it even partially. And of course, once a user has been successfully fooled into thinking that they are in a conversation, the question arises of how much sense it makes to tell them they're not.

The issue here is a conceptual one, which Alan Turing raised in a 1950 paper published in the philosophy journal *Mind*: if you could not tell whether your messages on a computer terminal were being answered by a person or a machine, why regard the answering behaviour as intelligent only if a person turned out to be involved, while denying it if a computer had composed the answers? Why should the computer not be credited with intelligence?

In 1966, Joseph Weizenbaum highlighted the issue by (unintentionally) demonstrating that the implicit test was much too easy for a machine to pass. He wrote a program called ELIZA which looked for patterns and keywords in input sentences, and applied certain simple operations, based on a script, to produce outputs depending on the inputs. The most famous script for it was known as DOCTOR. It made ELIZA simulate a Rogerian therapist by turning the user's inputs around to make questions. If the user mentioned anything being the same as anything else, the DOCTOR script might make ELIZA ask 'In what way?'; any mention of parents would trigger something like 'Tell me more about your parents'; and so on. It faked linguistic responses by simply replacing certain patterns spotted in word sequences typed by the user. And to Weizenbaum's astonishment, some people who tried it began to act as if they really were having an intimate and useful conversation with an intelligent entity.

ELIZA was written in 1966, only twenty years after the announcement of ENIAC, the first general-purpose electronic computer, and long before the development of microprocessors or personal computers. It thus needed very little memory to run. In fact its resource demands are so meagre that a version of it is embedded as an Easter egg inside the Emacs text editor, supplied free with most Unix, Linux, and Mac OS systems. (It is invoked by typing 'M–x doctor'. The ELIZA experiment reveals that our test for machine intelligence had better not be based on anything as easy as convincing an ordinary human that they are having a conversation.

HAL, of course, does not just look for keywords in Dave Bowman's utterances and transform them into suitable rejoinders to keep him talking. The chilling thing about HAL's responding to 'What's the problem?' that I mentioned at the beginning of the chapter ('I think you know what the problem is just as well as I do') is that it indicates that it knows the answer to Dave's question, but also sees him as an intelligent entity with mental states like beliefs and knowledge, and has formed an opinion concerning what he probably knows, and can compare his probable level of understanding with its own, and can respond to a question by expressing a conjecture about Dave's ability to answer it. This suggests true interaction of independent intelligent minds.

I'm actually not sure a machine could ever give evidence of true general intelligence other than through sophisticated handling of language. The kinds of nonlinguistic but putatively intelligent feats by computers that are beginning to get attention in the press under the heading of 'artificial intelligence' do not seem to me to be good examples of intelligent behaviour.

AlphaGo is a computer program that has proved it can beat any human player of Go, an extremely complex territory-capture strategy game played with stones on a board of nineteen by nineteen squares. But playing Go is all it can do, and it isn't even aware that it is playing. Mechanically and repetitively, it follows a built-in strategy of searching a gigantic tree of possible move sequences, annotated at each branching point with indications of the probability of winning if you go down that branch. It can't follow all legal game continuations from the current board configuration, taking note at each stage of how many of the games at that stage result in a win; there are too many even for a computer. The universe would end long before the search was over. But it takes a large random sample of them, considering vastly more possible games than any human could, and stashes away every useful piece of knowledge about what is discovered in the process.

It wins by exploiting incredible speed and massive quantities of memory – and of course being immune to fatigue and foreboding. There is no skill or grace or sensing of the opponent's strategy; AlphaGo doesn't even know that there is an opponent, only that certain moves are entered and must be responded to. Indeed, the creators found that the best way to create an even more adept program was to supply no initial strategy instructions at all, and simply let the machine learn what works by playing millions of games against itself. (Humans can't do that, but a computer's working memory can be divided into two separate areas that aren't allowed access to each other's workings.) AlphaGo's activities illustrate blazingly fast and tireless automatic instruction-following, not intelligence in anything like the normal sense.

Just to take one example, a human will decide when to resign from a game when they see they are doomed to lose (it's rude to waste the opponent's time), but AlphaGo has to be told when to resign (it bows out if its calculable probability of winning ever falls below 20%). The programmers wrote in the instruction because AlphaGo doesn't even know that there are such things as opponents, or that humans don't want their time wasted.

HAL's strategy for deciding what to say to Dave

cannot be anything like AlphaGo's strategy for playing Go or resigning. HAL can't be searching a random sample of all the conversations that could proceed from 'Open the pod bay doors, HAL' to see where they go. What would be the way to choose between conversational moves? Turns in a conversation are not like moving a stone from one square to another to alter winning probability; complex utterances with their own internal structure are designed to convey a specific meaning, with complex communicative goals relating to influencing or eliciting the interlocutor's state of mind. Utterances are chosen by reference to the content of all the previous utterances and all current real-world knowledge, including the potential implications of the most recent utterances by the other party in the context, and how relevant those potential implications are.

### *What Real Natural Language Processing Would Involve*

What would be involved in trying to write a computer program that would not just pick uncomprehending responses of a script like ELIZA, but would show the beginnings of the kind of genuine linguistic intelligence that HAL so chillingly exhibits?

It would depend on full grammatical description of the language. For concreteness, let's consider the specific case of providing answers from a database for an unlimited range of English questions, and consider what our system will need, given what it has to accomplish.

We'll need a list of all the words in English – tens of thousands of them, together with some representation of their meanings and all the grammatically significant information about them. For each word in the question, we'll have to figure out what category it belongs to. Computational linguists call this tagging. It is not a trivial matter of looking in a dictionary, because huge numbers of words belong to more than one category, and what is needed is the right one for the context. This will probably call for reference to statistical frequencies for frequently co-occurring word sequences.

Some provision will be needed for coping with novel words that the system has not previously seen, and guessing their category. It is a very interesting fact that when you encounter a sentence with a truly alien word about which you know nothing, you still take it in and understand it as English. If you read *My scurrop is capable of troodling a bivit*, you know what you've been told: you have learned that bivits can be troodled, and that my scurrop can accomplish this. You don't know what bivits are, or what a scurrop looks like, or what happens when you troodle something; but those are not questions about English; they're about bivits and scurrops and troodling. Our knowledge of grammar is independent of our knowledge of words: we can understand a sentence containing a word we don't know, and ideally a computer reconstruction of sentence processing should mimic that ability.

Then the tagged sequence of words must be used to figure out the most plausible grammatically permissible syntactic structure that it could be an instance of. And we hit another problem: some sequences of words have more than one permissible structure. One famous example (due to the machine translation pioneer Anthony Oettinger) is *Time flies like an arrow*. As a metaphorical way of saying that time passes very rapidly it has *time* tagged as a noun and *flies* as a verb. As a statement about the preferences of imaginary creatures called time flies, it has *flies* as a plural noun, *time* as a modifier, and *like* as a verb. Figure 2a and Figure 2b show the contrast.

An effective parser will need to be paired with a database of probabilities to help it guess which structures and meanings are most plausible for ambiguous strings of words. The alternative would be a huge stock of encyclopaedia information about the world, and ways of reasoning about it. Humans have exactly that, but modelling it with a machine would probably be much harder than relying on probabilities of sequences of words (only future research can determine whether I'm right about that).

Just guessing that Figure 2a is the more plausible one would call for knowing that there's no such animal as a time fly; that arrows travel at high speed; that *like an arrow* is a common simile for characterizing rapid travel; that time is sometimes conceptualized as moving past us; and so on. And (as Oettinger noted) *Fruit flies like a banana* has the same two possible structures, but it is the second (with *fruit flies* as a noun phrase and *like* as a verb meaning 'enjoy') that is more plausible. (He also notes that there is a third structure and meaning for *Time flies like an arrow*. I'll leave it as a puzzle for you to spot that.)

When the syntactic processing is done, an explicit representation must be built for the most likely literal meaning corresponding to the syntactic structure that the parser has constructed. This is another major theoretical task involving many unsolved problems. (I can't resist giving you one random example of such problems. *I ate the enormous banana* means that I ate the unique banana

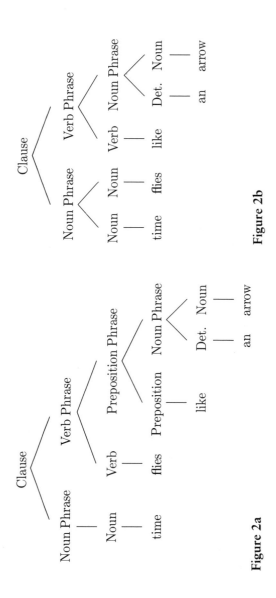

**Figure 2a**

**Figure 2b**

117

that you can identify by reference to its enormous size. But *I ate the occasional banana* is totally different. It doesn't mean I ate the unique banana that you can identify by reference to its being occasional. It means I ate bananas from time to time. What on earth is going on there? Thousands of such difficult puzzles in semantics await.)

Then the program must compare the literal meaning with what has been established by other sentences earlier in the conversation and compute the conclusions that should be drawn given what is relevant in the present context. This is pragmatics, perhaps the hardest part of the overall task. Humans are fantastically clever in this respect, having developed their skills over their entire lifetimes. To them it seems like just 'common sense'. Without such common sense you cannot even solve simple puzzles about what pronouns refer to. Imagine someone saying this on the phone to someone working for a courier company:

*I was in the shower when your delivery man tried to deliver a package to my flat yesterday. Can I have it delivered tomorrow?*

Instantly you know that *it* refers to the package. Not to my flat (though *my flat* is the most recent noun phrase before the pronoun), and not to the shower (though *the shower* is a salient noun phrase in the main clause rather than in the subordinate clause *your delivery man tried to deliver a package to my flat yesterday*). But how can a computer figure out such things if the pronoun *it* simply means 'the non-human entity just referred or alluded to'?

Once it is completely clear what should be understood from the question that the user has asked, we get to the crucial step that people working on database access call 'the back end': finding the answer. A representation of the conveyed meaning of the sentence in its context, with all ambiguities removed, must be used as the basis for extracting an answer from the appropriate database. This could be a process of some complexity, but let's assume that the answer can be found and presented in the system's own meaning representation system, so we can proceed to the final step the user will probably expect: phrasing the answer in English. A user would be rather disappointed to ask the computer a question in English like 'Who's the head of the College of Natural Sciences at the moment?' and receive something looking like this:

```
<EmpNo(849671-4), Keyname(Smith),
Title(Prof), StartDate(20130701), End
Date(NULL), JobTitle(HeadCollNatSci),
Forename(Mary)>
```

119

It would seem a lot friendlier if it were expressed as 'It's Professor Mary Smith.' So linguists and computer scientists will need to write a program that takes the information to be conveyed to the interlocutor and composes a sentence that expresses that meaning in a reasonable way that is appropriate to the context. This will be another extraordinarily difficult task, involving everything that falls within linguistics, not just grammar and semantics but also pragmatic concerns like politeness and level of formality.

The relevance of this anatomizing of the operation of an imaginary computerized question-answering system is that **all** of the steps will call for experts in linguistics. Getting computers to understand ordinary English (or text in any other human language) is the clearest and ultimately most important area in which we will come to appreciate the critical importance of linguistics.

# Conclusion

In this short survey I have been able to discuss only a small number of illustrations of the importance of scientific investigation of language. I know of linguists, psycholinguists, sociolinguists, and computational linguists who are involved in practical projects of dozens of different kinds: dictionary compilation; manuscript decipherment; speech synthesis; clarification of legal language; language planning; automatic text summarizing; brand name invention; forensic tweet analysis; language course design; machine translation; dialogue design for phone-answering systems; writing system development for hitherto unwritten languages; treatment for aphasic patients (people whose brain damage or disease has impaired their language use) . . . and I could go on.

The work of linguistics ranges from subfields

clearly falling within the humanities through descriptive social science to purely scientific investigation. But it is important that applications draw on all parts of this range at once. For example, attempting to ascertain the true authorship of disputed works by close study of writing style is a humanities project falling very much within the purview of the English department, but it was a computational linguist in a computer science department, Patrick Juola of Duquesne University, who unmasked the detective fiction writer Robert Galbraith in 2013 as actually being J.K. Rowling.

Likewise, mapping dialect locations is merely an aspect of descriptive human geography, but it has a new application now. Professor Simon King at the University of Edinburgh is systematically banking samples of speech from particular dialect areas in the United Kingdom so that speech synthesizers can be trained to produce local accents. The aim is to make it possible for patients with motor neurone disease, after their speech musculature has become disabled, to go on communicating in the accent to which they and their family are accustomed.

Style analysts, dialectologists, phoneticians, and other linguists do not generally start their investigations with a view to generating practical applications. They simply want to find certain things out. Relations between pure research and its applications are well known to be quite unpredictable: the discoverers of penicillin, X-rays, microwave cooking, and the not-too-sticky adhesive of Post-It notes were not looking for the things they happened to find. The linguistic sciences are devoted to studying language simply because it is so interesting. But they are studying a quintessentially distinctive human ability that is intimately linked to early childhood development, the functioning of the mind, the intricacies of social life, the proper functioning of the legal system, the teaching of languages, and many other things. Applications gradually emerge, and in my view we have so far seen only the very beginnings of them.

Nobody doubts that language is centrally important to human life. And to the extent that language is important, linguistics matters to all of us, probably in more ways than we can currently perceive.

# Notes on Further Reading

### Chapter 1 What Makes Us Human

Ambrose Bierce: See the entry for 'Man' in *The Devil's Dictionary* (originally 1911); quoted from *The Enlarged Devil's Dictionary*, ed. by E.J. Hopkins (Victor Gollancz, 1967), p. 193.

100,000 or 200,000 years: Daniel Everett, in *How Language Began: The Story of Humanity's Greatest Invention* (Profile Books, 2017), reckons it was more like a million.

Rico the collie: Juliane Kaminski, Josep Call, and Julia Fischer, 'Word learning in a domestic dog: evidence for "fast mapping"', *Science* **304.5677** (11 June 2004), 1682–3, and, on pp. 1605–6 of the same issue, Paul Bloom, 'Can a dog learn a word?'

7,000 languages: Raymond G. Gordon, Jr. (ed.), *Ethnologue: Languages of the World* (15th edition, SIL International, 2005). See also Stephen R. Anderson,

# Notes on Further Reading

*Languages: A Very Short Introduction* (Oxford University Press, 2012).

Hawaiian language: Samuel H. Elbert and Mary Kawena Pukui, *Hawaiian Grammar* (University of Hawaii Press, 1979); Mary Kawena Pukui and Samuel H. Elbert, *Hawaiian Dictionary* (University of Hawaii Press, 1986).

Diversity of word order: Desmond C. Derbyshire and Geoffrey K. Pullum, 'Object initial languages', *International Journal of American Linguistics* **47.3** (1981), 192–214.

## Chapter 2 How Sentences Work

Harold Evans: *Do I Make Myself Clear?* (Little, Brown and Company, 2017), p. 3.

Bullokar's grammar: William Bullokar, *Pamphlet for Grammar* (Henry Denham, 1586).

Lily's grammar: William Lily et al., *Rudimenta Grammatices* (Oxford, c. 1509).

American linguists: Charles C. Fries, *The Teaching of the English Language* (Thomas Nelson, 1927); Leonard Bloomfield, *Language* (Holt, 1933); Robert A. Hall Jr., *Leave Your Language Alone!* (Linguistica Press, 1950).

Vampire fans: Bram Stoker, *Dracula* (Archibald Constable and Company, 1897).

Getting the data wrong: For excellent guidance on hundreds of controversies concerning contemporary English usage, see the excellent *Merriam-Webster's Dictionary of English Usage* (Merriam-Webster, 1994).

Maine court case: O'Connor v. Oakhurst Dairy, No. 16-1901 (1st Cir. 2017). See Jason Eisner's post 'Court fight over Oxford commas and asyndetic lists' on Language Log, 19 March 2017 (http://languagelog.ldc.upenn.edu/nll/?p=31653).

### Chapter 3 Words, Meaning, and Thought

Untranslatable words: For a recent list (among thousands of similar posts) see Rocket Language Blog, 27 November 2016, by Andrea Reisenauer (https://www.rocketlanguages.com/blog/20-of-the-worlds-most-beautiful-untranslatable-words/).

Conventional implicatures: The term is used here in the sense developed by Christopher Potts in *The Logic of Conventional Implicatures* (Oxford University Press, 2005). Potts redefines a term introduced earlier by the philosopher H. Paul Grice (*Studies in the Way of Words*, Harvard University Press, 1989).

Libel law: Geoffrey K. Pullum, 'The linguistics of defamation' and 'Trenchmouth comes to Trumpington Street', Chapters 12 and 13 of my *The Great Eskimo Vocabulary Hoax and Other Irreverent Essays on the Study of Language* (University of Chicago Press, 1991), 92–99, 100–10. See also Roger Shuy, *The Language of Defamation Cases* (Oxford University Press, 2010).

# Notes on Further Reading

Eskimoan: The Eskimoan language family comprises four Yupik languages (Siberian Yupik, Central Alaskan Yupik, Naukan, and Alutiiq) and four Inuit languages (Inupiaq, Inuvialuktun, Inuktitut, and Greenlandic or Kalaallisut).

Laura Martin: '"Eskimo words for snow": a case study in the genesis and decay of an anthropological example', *American Anthropologist* **88.2** (1986), 418–23.

Eskimo 'hoax': Geoffrey K. Pullum, 'The great Eskimo vocabulary hoax': Chapter 19 of my *The Great Eskimo Vocabulary Hoax*, 159–71.

Mark Seidenberg on reading: *Language at the Speed of Sight: How We Read, Why So Many Can't, and What Can Be Done About It* (Basic Books, 2017).

## *Chapter 4 Language and Social Life*

Trayvon Martin and Rachel Jeantel: John R. Rickford and Sharese King, 'Language and linguistics on trial: hearing Rachel Jeantel (and other vernacular speakers) in the courtroom and beyond', *Language* **92.4** (2016), 948–88.

William Labov on speech and class: *The Social Stratification of English in New York City* (Center for Applied Linguistics, 1966).

Labov on AAVE: 'Contraction, deletion, and inherent variability in the English copula', *Language* **45.4** (1969), 715–76; 'The logic of nonstandard English', in *Language*

# Notes on Further Reading

*and Poverty: Perspectives on a Theme*, ed. by Frederick Williams (Markham, 1971), 153–89.

Syntactic rules of AAVE: Geoffrey K. Pullum, 'African American English is not standard English with mistakes', in *The Workings of Language: From Prescriptions to Perspectives*, ed. by Rebecca S. Wheeler (Praeger, 1999), 39–58.

W. Sidney Allen on trusting informants: See Allen's 1957 inaugural lecture, published as 'On the linguistic study of languages', in *Five Inaugural Lectures*, ed. by Peter D. Strevens (Oxford University Press, 1966), 3–26; see pp. 18–19.

Nembe and Kalabari: Hans Wolff, 'Intelligibility and inter-ethnic attitudes', *Anthropological Linguistics* **1.3** (1959): 34–41. Reprinted as Chapter 46 of *Language in Culture and Society*, ed. by Dell Hymes (Harper & Row, 1964), 440–5; see p. 442.

Klima and Bellugi: For an overview of some of the research of Edward Klima and Ursula Bellugi on sign languages, see *The Signs of Language* (Harvard University Press, 1979).

Nim Chimpsky: The 2011 British documentary *Project Nim* is particularly worth watching in connection with the failure of efforts to teach sign language to chimpanzees.

# Notes on Further Reading

### Chapter 5 Machines That Understand Us

HAL 9000 and Dave Bowman: The film *2001: A Space Odyssey* (1968) was directed by Stanley Kubrick. The novel by Arthur C. Clarke was developed contemporaneously.

Mark Steedman: 'On becoming a discipline', *Computational Linguistics* **34** (2008), 137–44; see p. 143.

Facebook chatbots: Kevin Maney, 'How Facebook's AI bots learned their own language and how to lie', *Newsweek*, 5 August 2017.

Alan Turing on intelligence: 'Computing machinery and intelligence', *Mind* **90.236** (1950), 433–60.

Joseph Weizenbaum and ELIZA: 'ELIZA – a computer program for the study of natural language communication between man and machine', *Communications of the ACM*, **9.1** (1966), 36–45.

*Time flies*: Anthony G. Oettinger,'The uses of computing in science', *Scientific American* **215.3** (1966), 160–75; see p. 168.

# Index

*2001: A Space Odyssey* (film and novel), 83–5, 128

adjective, 28, 43–4, 61–2
Africa, 2, 77
African American Vernacular English (AAVE), 66–9, 72, 72–4, 127–8
agreement, grammatical, 27
alarm calls, 6
Alexa, 85
algorithms, 84–5, 89, 92
Allen, W. Sidney, 75, 128
Allo (app), 85
alphabet, 17, 64, 80
AlphaGo (computer program), 111–12
ambiguity, 21, 60, 115
America, United States of, vii, 26, 30, 67, 72, 94–100
*American Anthropologist* (journal), 49
American Indian languages, 26

American Sign Language (ASL), 79–82
animals, 2, 4, 6
anthropology, 15, 48, 76
Apache, Plains, 9
apes *see* primates
aphasia, 64, 121–2
applications of research, 123
Arabic language, 70–1
Aramaic language, Galilean, 9
asyndetic coordination, 33–4
Australia, 9
authorship identification, 122
automatic text summarizing, 121
auxiliary verb, 73, 90

back end (database), 119
Bayes' theorem, 36–8
Belgium, 8
Bellugi, Ursula, 79, 128
Bible translation, 15
Bierce, Ambrose, 2, 124
birds, 24, 29

# Index

Bloom, Paul, 7, 124
Bowman, Dave, 83–4, 110
brain, 13, 58–9, 63, 98, 121
brand name invention, 121
Brazil, 15–16
Bullokar, William, 22, 125
Bush, George W., 105
*but*, 42

Canada, 2, 48, 51
casual speech, 75
category (grammatical), 97
chainsaw safety, 22–3
chatbots, 90–2
chemotherapy, 63
China, 94
clauses,
  interrogative, 95–6
  main, 119
  relative, 61, 98
  subordinate, 29, 81, 119
cognition, 20, 44
colour words, 56–7
communication, 4–5, 91
computational linguistics,
  106, 114, 121
computers, 83–4, 98, 101–20
conjunction *see* coordinator
connotation, 43
constituent (syntactic), 97
constraints, grammatical,
  24–5, 62
conventional implicature, 43,
  126
conversational implicature,
  45
coordination, 32–4
coordinator, 24–5, 33
copula (*be*), omission of, 72
Cornish language, 11

Cortana, 85
creole languages, 69, 82
Cretaceous period, 29
culture, 40, 48–9

*damn*, 42–3
Danish language, 42
data storage, 86
defamation, 45–6, 126
definite article, 61
dementia, 63
Denmark, 42
denotation, 41–3, 45
Derbyshire, Desmond C.,
  15–17, 125
dialects, 8, 52, 66–7, 69–71,
  73, 75–7, 82, 122
dialogue design, 121
dictionary making, 121
dinosaurs, 29–30
DOCTOR (computer script),
  109–10
dogs, 6
Doyle, Sir Arthur Conan,
  25
*Dracula*, 27, 125
Dutch language, 8
dyslexia, 63

Easter eggs, 85–6
Edinburgh, University of, viii,
  122
education, 23, 25, 30, 63–5
Eisner, Jason, 36, 126
Elbert, Samuel, 10, 125
electroencephalography, 59
ELIZA (computer program),
  109–10, 113, 128
emotion, 5, 44
engineering, 103, 107

131

# Index

English language, 9, 18, 21–3, 25–6, 29, 30, 36, 39, 46, 52, 69, 73, 83, 114–15, 119–20
ENIAC (computer), 109
Eskimo vocabulary hoax, 49, 127
Eskimoan languages, 48–55, 127
ethnic slurs, 44
Eurasia, 2
Evans, Sir Harold, 19, 125
Everett, Daniel L., 124
evolution, 1, 37, 79
eye-tracking, 59

Facebook, 90
fast mapping, 7, 124
First Circuit, US Court of Appeals, 32
Flemish language, 8
forensic linguistics, 121
French language, 13, 24, 47

Galbraith, Robert, 122
George III, 30
German language, 46
GitHub, 97
Gmail, 90
Go (game), 111
Google, 85, 87, 89–90, 92–5, 101
grammar, 19–30, 57–8, 69, 72, 84, 89, 120
grammaticality 24–5
Greek language, 18, 74–5
Guyana, 15

HAL (computer), 83–4, 110, 112–13, 128

Hawaii, 94
Hawaii, University of, 11
Hawaiian language, 10–11, 125
hearsay marker, 53–4
Hebrew language, 11
Hindi language, 8
Hixkaryana language, 15–17
Hungarian language, 73
hypotheses, 55–6

iconicity, 80–1
India, 8
inflection, 52–5, 74
influentiality ranking, 88
innuendo see conversational implicature
intelligibility, 76–8
interrogative clauses see clauses
Inuit language, 48
Inuktitut language, 51
iPhone, 85
Irish language, 11
Italian language, 8, 92

Japanese language, 92
Jeantel, Rachel, 66–8, 74, 127
Jesus, 9
jokes, 50
journalists, 91
Juola, Patrick, 122

Kalabari language, 77–8, 128
King, Sharese, 67, 127
King, Simon, 122
Klima, Edward, 79, 128
Koko (gorilla), 81–2
Kweyol language, Haitian, 69

# Index

Labov, William, 71–2, 127
language,
  change in, 21, 26–7
  definition of, 2–3
  diversity of, 12–17
  extinction, 9–12
  learning and teaching of,
    12, 17, 48, 121
  low-prestige, 76
languages, number of, 8–9
Latin language, 18, 22
law, language and, 31–7, 45,
    66–9, 121
learning disabilities, 63
libel *see* defamation
Lily, William, 22, 125
linguistics, 3, 7, 10–12, 20,
    30, 36, 40, 51, 70–1, 78,
    102–3, 107–8, 120, 121,
    123
Linux, 110

Mac OS, 110
Madagascar, 14
Madison (Wisconsin), 64
Madrell, Ned, 11
main clauses *see* clauses
Maine, 31, 33, 35
Malagasy language, 14
Manx language, 11
Martin, Laura, 48–9, 127
Martin, Trayvon, 66–7,
    127
memory, 6, 120, 122
mental states, 83–4, 110
Merrill, Bob, 93
metaphor, 42, 115
metaphysics, 56
Mexico, 14, 95
Microsoft Word, 103, 105

*Mind* (philosophy journal),
    108
missionary work, 15
modifier (grammatical), 115
monkeys, 6
monotremes, 41
morphology, 13, 52–5
Morse code, 5
motor neurone disease, 122

natural language processing,
    101, 113
negation, 94
Nembe language, 77–8, 128
neurology, 64
neuroscience, 40
New Testament, 15
New York City, 71–2
New Zealand, 94
*Newsweek*, 91, 128
Ni'ihau, 10
Nim Chimpsky (chimpanzee),
    81–2, 128
nonstandard dialects, 66–9,
    75
North America, 9
noun, 28, 61–2, 97, 118
noun phrase, 97–8, 118

Oakhurst Dairy case, 31–5,
    126
object (grammatical), 28,
    81
Oettinger, Anthony, 115–16,
    128
onomatopoeia, 81
OSV (Object–Subject–Verb)
    languages, 16
OVS (Object–Verb–Subject)
    languages, 13, 16

# Index

palaeontology, 29
parsing, 84, 115
Pennsylvania, University of, 71
perjury, 45
philosophy, 13–14, 40
phonetics, 5, 12, 122
phonics, 65
phonology, 13, 17, 19, 69, 80
physiotherapy, 64
postbases, 52–5
pragmatics, 5, 13, 20, 45–7, 58, 118, 120
prairie dogs, 6
preposition, 23, 27, 28
primates, 1, 81
probability, 37–8, 62, 115–6
processing (of sentences or utterances), 63, 84, 116
pronoun, 118
proofreading, 103, 108
psycholinguistics, 57, 59, 63–5, 121
psychology, 40, 76
Pukui, Margaret Kawena, 10, 125
punctuation, 32–5, 87, 126

question-answering, 93

reading, 61, 64–5, 127
relative clauses *see* clauses
Rickford, John, 67, 127
Rico (border collie), 6–7, 124
robots, 84, 108
Romance languages, 8
Rowling, J.K., 122
rules, grammatical, 24–5, 27, 37, 62
Russian language, 73

Sadock, Jerry, viii
Sapir–Whorf hypothesis, 55–6
Scholastic Aptitude Test (SAT), 30
Scots language, 8
Seidenberg, Mark, 64–5, 127
semantics, 13, 17, 20, 41–7, 57–8, 62, 81, 115–16, 118, 120
sentence, 5, 19–20, 23, 58–60, 107
sign languages, 79–82
Siri, 85
size adjectives, 43–4
slips of the tongue, 75
smartphones, 84–6
snow, words for, 48–52, 54–5
social class, 72
sociolinguistics, 71–8, 121
South America, 9, 15
SOV (Subject–Object–Verb) languages, 13, 21
Spanish language, 69, 92
speech recognition, 84
speech sounds, 5, 12, 17, 58, 64
speech synthesis, 121–2
speech therapy, 64
spelling, 80, 89, 104, 106
standard English, 69, 74
Stanford University, 67
*Star Trek*, 47
statistics, 85–6, 89
Steedman, Mark, viii, 87, 128
Streisand, Barbra, 93
style, 122

# Index

Styne, Jule, 93
subject (grammatical), 28, 81, 90
subordinate clauses *see* clauses
Summer Institute of Linguistics, 15
SVO (Subject–Verb–Object) languages, 13–14, 17, 21
Swedish language, 42
syndetic coordination, 33
syndetic coordination, 33–5
syntax, 13, 14–17, 20, 80, 101, 116

tagging, 114
testability, 56
therapy, 63, 109
thought, 3–5, 17, 40, 44, 58
translating and interpreting, 39–47, 69, 81
tree diagram, 97–8, 111
truth conditions, 41–2
Tunisian language, 70–1, 76
Turing, Alan, 108, 128
Tzotzil language, 14

understanding sentences, 85–90
United Kingdom, 122
University College London, 14
Unix, 110
Urdu language, 8
URL (Uniform Resource Locator), 87, 95
Utah, 30
Uzbekistan, 89

verb, 55, 62, 81
verb phrase, 97
Vienna, 49
vocabulary size, 51
VOS (Verb–Object–Subject) languages, 13
VSO (Verb–Subject–Object) languages, 13

*Wall Street Journal*, 106
Washoe (chimpanzee), 81–2
Weizenbaum, Joseph, 109, 128
Wells, H.G., 25
Welsh language, 11
West Greenlandic Inuit language (Kalaallisut), 51–5
Wheeler, Rebecca, viii, 128
Wilde, Oscar, 103
Wisconsin, University of, 64
Wolff, Hans, 77, 128
word processing, 103, 105, 107–8
words, 19–20, 57–8, 60, 115
words, untranslatable, 39–47, 126
writing systems, 17, 64, 80, 121
Wycliffe Bible Translators, 15

York, University of, viii
Yupik language, 48

Zambia, 94
Zimmerman, George, 67
zoology, 1, 29